CHURCH CARPENTRY

CHURCH CARPENTRY

A Study based on Essex examples

Cecil A. Hewett

PHILLIMORE

1982

Published by
PHILLIMORE & CO. LTD.
London and Chichester

Head Office: Shopwyke Hall,
Chichester, Sussex, England

ISBN 0 85033 397 0

Printed and bound in Great Britain by
UNWIN BROTHERS LIMITED
at the Gresham Press, Old Woking, Surrey

CONTENTS

LIST OF PLATES

(between pages 44 and 45)

Photographs by Frank Joel

LIST OF FIGURES

ROOFS

DOORS

ACKNOWLEDGEMENTS

My grateful thanks are due to the many Rectors and Vicars associated with the churches herein described, also to my wife and my eldest son, for routing the numerous long journeys involved, and for continual assistance with the compilation of this text.

INTRODUCTION

The county of Essex has 410 ancient parishes, and according to the Inventory of the Royal Commission on Historic Monuments, 350 of these retain their ancient churches either wholly, or in part. Since the Royal Commission visited the county some churches have been demolished, and several ruined examples also exist upon private ground, but since they have no carpentry these have not been included.

The author has found it necessary to define church carpentry as roofs, belfries and spires, porches and door leaves; smaller works such as screens, pulpits, parish chests, lecterns and sanctuary rails have been regarded as furnishings rather than as carpentry, and left for the detailed examination of others. The examples in these categories that best illustrate the historical succession and its changing techniques are described and illustrated in their historical order, but are kept in separate categories for the purpose. As a result there is a section of the text that traces the course of developments in roof-framing, of naves, chancels, aisles and chapels and transepts; and similar sections on the other categories of framing. The examples selected for detailed treatment are necessarily few, and only comprise those relevant to the purpose; the remaining examples of the types found are listed under their parish names in the final gazetteer.

It seems that no previous publication has attempted to analyse the hundreds of works of carpentry that these churches embody, and in view of the numerous books dealing with church craftsmanship this lack of information is difficult to explain. It is hoped that this limited essay will make some amends for this lack of literature, and it may possibly provide a companion volume to Sir Nikolaus Pevsner's Essex work. More than a decade of fruitful studies has elapsed since this text was first prepared, and the date limits of the periods of English architectural history have altered permanently in that time. The re-examination of these four hundred churches has not proved possible, and the text has, therefore, been revised sufficiently to ensure that it is nowhere in conflict with views that now obtain.

C. A. HEWETT
1980

Chapter One

Developments during the Romanesque

Of the many churches examined in order that this carpentry assessment could be made, a high proportion embody evidence of their Romanesque origins, yet from a total exceeding four hundred, only seven retain any timbering that can easily be seen and typologically reconciled with carpenters' work of that period. Reasons for this are numerous, not least the unceasing urge to improve and enhance the church, which, more than any other rural building, was always an object for patronage and for the expression of parochial prosperity. It is sometimes difficult to assign works of carpentry to the accepted periods of English architecture, which were defined by reference to works of masonry; but these periods are adhered to in this book, and will make use of architectural knowledge already possessed by the reader. The seven churches will be described in what appears to be their historical succession; two Saxon ones first, followed by five Norman examples under the appropriate dynastic divisions of the English Romanesque period.

The Anglo-Saxon Period (A.D. 449 to 1066)

Unlikely though they seem, some examples of carpentry from this period have survived in Essex: the walls of St. Andrew at Greensted-juxta-Ongar, the north door and four window frames designed to take glazing at St. Botolph's, Hadstock, and the north door of St. Mary's at Buttsbury. The unique building among these is the log-walled church of St. Andrew at Greensted, which owes its survival to its apparently unquestionable association with St. Edmund, a king of the East Saxons who was martyred by the Danes in 870. St. Edmund's remains were transferred in 1013 from London to Bedriceworth, afterwards called Bury St. Edmunds. This event was recorded by a monk of Bury St. Edmunds in a document (B.M. Add. MS. 14847, f.20 and *V.C.H.*, 1956, 60; *see* Hewett, 1980, 5) that has not been dated with certainty, but which appears to have been no later than *c.* 1300 and may date from *c.* 1100. According to various accounts written before the 'restoration' of 1849, which was undertaken by the Reverend P. W. Ray, this church had survived almost intact until his time. Little, however, escaped his restoration, and much that was of supreme interest was destroyed, such as the greater part of the original west gable, which must have contained vital evidence as to the roof construction. What remains today is the greater part of the north and south walls, together with two areas of the west gable. The number of half-logs in these walls is uncertain because Ray renewed some and moved others to different places, but most seem to be the originals, which consistently comprise small oaks of less than a century's growth. These were split into halves and reared with their curved surfaces outwards upon a groundsill, and fitting into a grooved top plate; their edges were slightly flattened and grooved to receive fillets, in order to exclude dampness and draughts. Unfortunately, the contemporary accounts do not agree with one another, and Ray himself asserts that the western gable was 'of two layers of planks fastened together with treenails'; but no clear evidence of this has survived. The top plates were renewed at this time, and fitted in the curious way illustrated in Fig. 1, which seems unnecessarily complex, and may for that reason represent the original method. Other facts concerning this church can be found in the index of parishes, p. 110. (*See also* Hewett, 1980, 5-13.)

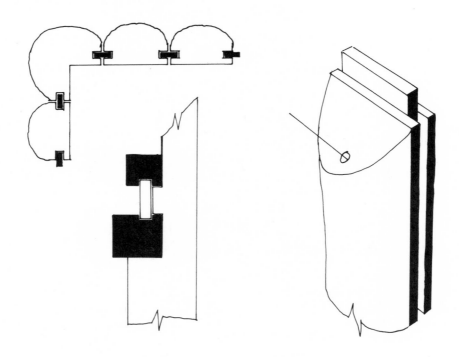

Fig. 1.   9th-century log church at Greensted-juxta-Ongar

Concerning Hadstock, it appears that King Cnut built a minster of 'stone and lime' after defeating Edmund Ironside at the battle of Assandun in 1016, and that there are grounds for identifying this church with his minster, which was built to commemorate those slain (Dr. W. Rodwell, 1976, 69). The north door of the church is widely known (see p. 78), but attention was first directed to its mid-wall window frames by Dr. H. M. Taylor (H. M. and J. Taylor, 1965, 274). These seem to be associated with glazing, and fragmentary iron saddle-bars remain affixed to them. (*See also* pp. 110-111, 116 and 135.)

Chapter Two

Roof Framing

I

During: The Norman Period, c. 1050–c. 1150

The parish of Chipping Ongar has an unusually complete Norman village church dedicated to St. Martin of Tours. It was ascribed by the Royal Commission to the end of the 11th century, between *c.* 1080 and *c.* 1100. It is a building rich in historic carpentry, but for the present purpose the chancel is of the greatest interest.

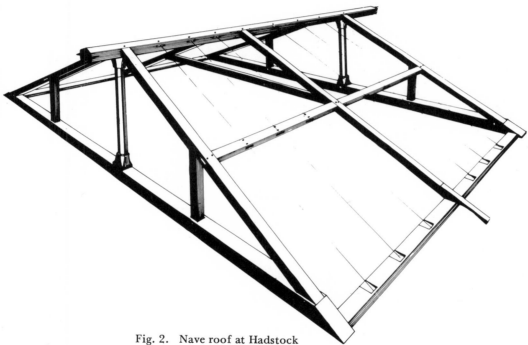

Fig. 2. Nave roof at Hadstock

As it exists now it is covered by a hybrid of four different roof systems, the most recent of which has pendants, dated 'WS 1643'. This most recent and dated frame was contrived to support the remains of three far more ancient systems, parts of which are still visible. The two oldest types are both illustrated in Fig. 3, at 'a' and 'b' respectively. At the left of the drawing, at 'a', is shown one rafter couple which is assembled in seven cants, and which represents the nine pairs of rafters at the western end close to the chancel arch. They all have vee struts above the collars and are jointed by barefaced lap dovetails and butt notchings, which are pegged through their inner faces. An exploded view of the butt-notched technique is shown at the left of the figure. At the centre of this chancel there are two rafter couples like that shown at 'b', with scissor braces that are trenched through the collars, dovetailed at their tops (barefaced lap dovetails) and, what is most important, notch-lapped at their lower ends. One of these lower, notched, joints is shown enlarged at the extreme right of the figure.

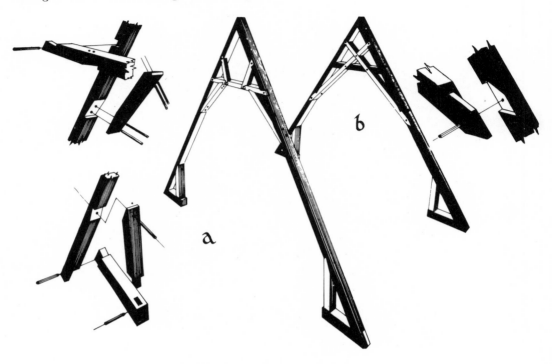

Fig. 3. Chipping Ongar: examples of the roof construction

Stanway church, dedicated to St. Albright, was ascribed by the Royal Commission in 1926 to sometime between *c.* 1125 and *c.* 1150. The nave roof at Stanway has one rafter couple that can be reconciled with such a dating, but owing to a drastic restoration all secondary members are missing, and only the empty notched-lap matrices can be seen. No illustration is warranted by this example.

A strange case among the five churches which have carpentry of this period is Roydon, where the church, dedicated to St. Peter, was dated by the Royal Commission to the early 13th century. The earliest feature visible today that supports this ascription is one renewed lancet window on the south side. The roof of the nave could, however, be ascribed to this or some earlier date. One bay of this roof is shown in Fig. 4, in which enough components have been omitted to clarify the construction. It is a tied roof with vee struts above its collars: the struts are notch-lapped into position, as are the upper ends of the ashlar pieces, while the collar braces are chase-tenoned and spiked, with iron, into place. The strongest evidence for the great age of this roof is provided by the crown posts, one of which can be seen in Plate I. These posts can be ascribed to between *c*. 1260 and *c*. 1280 by the mouldings of their capitals and bases; yet they are clearly an intrusion into the roof, doubtless inserted at a time when the latter was considered inadequate, or structurally weak.

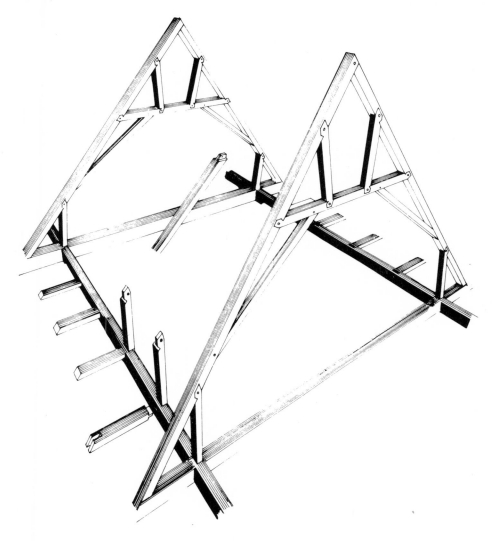

Fig. 4. Nave roof at Roydon

At the church of St. Mary Magdalene, East Ham, it is the apse lying to the east of the chancel which has retained its original roof, of which only the exterior cladding seems to have been renewed. It is illustrated, diagrammatically, in Figs. 5 and 6. The first is an exterior view and shows the numerous thick battens that were inserted between the rafters in rather an unsystematic and joggled order. These were probably fitted to facilitate the tying of thatch, in addition to providing extra stability for the rafters. The inset at the right shows the way in which the king posts were trenched to clasp the collars with their feet, and the ridge piece and rafters with their tops. Fig. 6 shows the partial outline of the masonry fabric, with windows and pilaster buttresses, together with a complete view of the five collar and king-post couples, which are shown in their spatial relationship to the semi-circular wall plate. This wall plate was made from 14 short lengths of 'compass timber' which were tenoned into the edges of the massive sole plates.

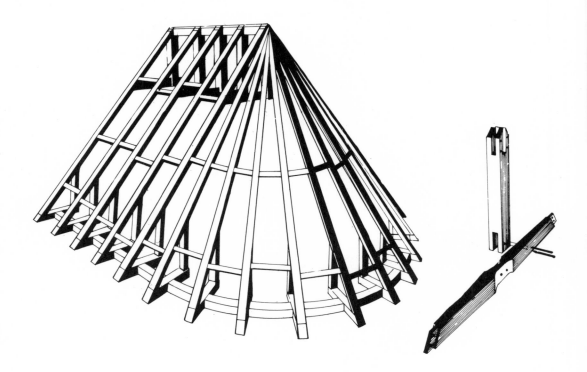

Fig. 5. Apse roof at East Ham: the framing

Waltham Abbey, dedicated to the Holy Cross, was founded as a collegiate church of secular canons in 1030; it was enlarged or refashioned by Earl Harold, and then consecrated in 1060. After this the usual vicissitudes befell it, until at the present time a small part survives as the parish church. The nave of the present church was built to the west of the original nave during the latter part of the reign of Henry I, and has been closely dated by Mr. S. E. Rigold to the decade 1120–30. The masonry is of a single build from east to west and from ground to eaves, where it was originally parapetted. An uncertain quantity of its original roof had survived until the early 19th century, when it was dismantled and its timbers used to produce a king-post roof that is inscribed 'LTW' and 'CP', and dated '1807'. At that time, insofar as may be discerned, the original tie beams were retained and the ceiling painted. The surviving timbers are not illustrated, but they were all cut for notched laps of the open variety, and indicate a roof in seven cants with double collars—all notched-lap-jointed and with a tie beam to every couple.

6

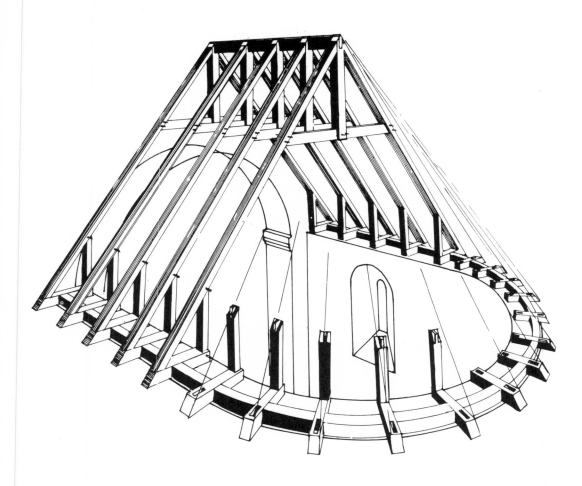

Fig. 6.   Apse roof at East Ham; a view

The four examples illustrated lack any datings other than those given for the carcases of masonry, in most cases by the Royal Commission, and extremely little substantiating evidence exists in the three forms generally accepted today: documentary evidence, dendrochronological evidence and carbon[14] measurements. The ascriptions made by the Commission do, however, provide guidance for the dating of the timber roofs, since the latter are unlikely to be older than the walls they crown; and where the carpentry can be reconciled with the masonry detail, the carcase dating can be taken as the greatest probable age for the timber-work. Several of the examples have carpentry that, in the light of present knowledge, seems almost contemporary but is in fact a little later than the general fabric of the church. These cases are the most difficult to explain, and they may have to await specific evidence from the alternative sources mentioned.

The rafter couples surviving at Chipping Ongar are of great interest and represent a roof of which only seven couples remain. These were designed as compressive arches beneath their collars, and jointed to resist extension above them and at their eaves. They exist at the least disturbed end of the chancel, and there is no reason not to assume that they date from the initial consecration of the church, late in the 11th century. A comparable roof that is jointed in the same way, at every joint, exists in Germany at the monastery church of Mittelzell, in Lake Constance, which has been dated by dendrochronology to 1235±3 years (R. Reuter, *Denkmalpflege*, 54). It is interesting to note that this date falls within the limits proposed by Deneux for such jointing, and has been determined by him from documentary evidence. (Hewett, Trans. Anc. Mons. Soc., 1969, 98.)

The east end of the Ongar chancel has been much altered, as the traces of blocked Norman windows testify, and as a probable result of this alteration the eastern half of the roof has been renewed. The existing east window was made *c.* 1300 according to the local information, and the seven western couples of trussed rafters can readily be ascribed to this date; but at the centre of the roof between the seven ancient couples and the seven 14th-century couples there are two couples with scissor braces. These two are of the type shown in Fig. 3 at 'b', and they can be dated to the early 13th century, since scissor braces were fitted with different joints during the late 13th century. Comparable roof couples framed together in this way are known to exist at Peterborough, where they may be survivals from the nave roof there, dating from between 1117 and 1190; and a further 81 couples of the type exist above the nave of Ely Cathedral, dating from the early 13th century.

The single rafter couple that survives at Stanway has apparently been re-used, and since it is no longer in its proper context it is difficult to determine whether it belonged to the original roof: however, that would be unlikely if scissors were fitted, since the church was ascribed to the early 12th century. The nave roof at Roydon is problematic, but it is not without comparable examples among the roofs shown by Deneux, although he does not, to my knowledge, show any that are identical (H. Deneux, 1947, No. D4554). Vee struts that are fitted with notched laps above collars like those at Roydon are shown by Deneux in the context of the Cistercian Abbey of Noirlac, which is dated by documentary evidence to between 1150 and 1160. (Trans. Anc. Mons. Society, 1969.) It is reasonable to assume that the Roydon roof is of the same age as the church, which the Royal Commission ascribed to 1200-1250, but archaeological examination of churches in Essex has consistently proved that they cannot be dated on the basis of the fabric visible today. Similar vee struts that are differently jointed are known to exist at Ely in the roof of the west range, which dates from *c.* 1190 (J. M. Fletcher & F. W. O. Haslop, 1970, 171-196).

The East Ham roof is remarkable, and difficult to compare with others, since so few 12th-century examples are known. It seems at the present time to be rare, having neither lap dovetails nor notched-lap joints, both of which occur most frequently during the Romanesque period. The structural device employed there is the bridled end joint shown in Fig. 5. The Waltham Abbey roof was predominantly notch-lapped, and would logically date from *c.* 1130 when the clerestory beneath it was finished, during the years of the Norman period. On this evidence, a variety of apparently concurrent carpenters' practices seems to have co-existed during this 100-year period. The use of king and ridge pieces is readily acceptable, but the appearance of seven-canted couples such as those at Ongar would be surprising if their date were confirmed, since this type of roof frame has recently been thought to derive from scissor-braced roofs, rather than precede them. Of the roof systems, not one stands out as being typical of the period (about which little can be learned),

8

but the examples differ to a sufficient extent to preclude the formulation of any single dogma. The predominant usage is of lap joints, either lap dovetails or notched laps, which are present in most of the surviving examples.

II

During: The Early English Period: c. 1150–c. 1250

This period saw the introduction, possibly at Wells, of a markedly English Gothic, and carpenters of the time continued to employ long bracing timbers that were halved through successive frame members, and secured at their ends in notched lap joints. Three buildings have been selected to represent the period.

The Abbey at Little Coggeshall still retains, intact, its capella-extra-muros, or chapel-without-the-walls. The latter has survived long periods of use as a farm building, and also a 19th-century restoration, without losing its Early English roof, comprising 25 rafter couples with collars and scissor braces, a pair of which is shown in Fig. 7. The recorded history of the Abbey indicates that this chapel would have been built during the time of Abbot Benedict (1218–1223), and the Royal Commission ascribed it more specifically to c. 1220.

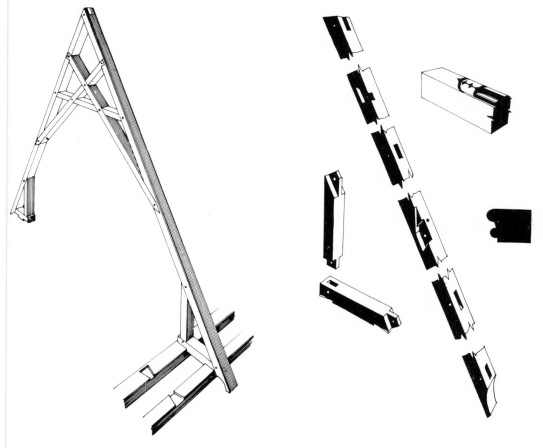

Fig. 7.   The capella-extra-muros at Little Coggeshall Abbey

The diagram at the right of Fig. 7 shows the joints used to assemble these couples, and the matrix shown third from the bottom of the rafter, which was the socket designed to hold the lower end of the scissor brace, is the joint which is most peculiar to this period. This is the 'secret' notched lap joint. The notch that was removed from the lap in order that it should resist withdrawal was cut so as to be invisible when the joint was assembled, and the object of this device was to increase the strength of the joint by avoiding any penetration of the notch to the visible face of the joint. (*Medieval Archaeology*, vol. XXII, 1978. 'The thirteenth-century roofs and floor of the Blackfriars Priory at Gloucester', pp. 105-122). A short length of the original wall plate has also survived, and its chamfer stop and sectional profile are both shown in the illustration. The lap dovetails were cut into the two wall plates to receive the sole pieces, and this technique is a feature of the same period in France.

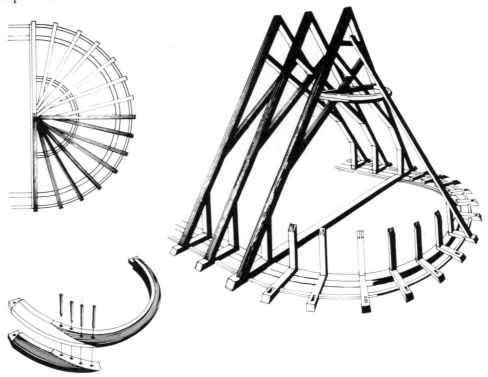

Fig. 8. The apse roof at Little Braxted

One other apse roof, that at Little Braxted church, is probably as old as the general fabric of the building, which was ascribed by the Royal Commission to the 12th century. This roof is shown in Fig. 8. The tie beam in the drawing is the diameter of the curve, and the rafter couples are scissor-braced without collars, except for the diametrical couple. This has two collars, one above the other, and in addition mounts the unique semicircular collar to support the converging rafters in the 'conoid' end of the roof. The way in which the rafters converge is shown in the plan at the left of the figure, and the construction of the compassed collar by

10

means of a splayed scarf is shown at the lower left. It is important to note that only tenoned end joints exist in this roof, in contrast to the preceding examples of scissor bracing, in which notched laps, either 'open' or 'secret', were used for their lower terminal joints.

The nave roof of the church at White Roding illustrates clearly the next development in roof-framing, which was the introduction of 'double-framing'—a technicality that warrants explanation. With the single exception of the East Ham example, all the roof systems described up to this point have been single-framed; that is, they were constructed in frames designed to span the distance between the two walls. These frames were held upright by the external cladding and were not otherwise connected. Thus single-framed roofing was framed—jointed—in only the transverse direction, while the later double-framing was jointed in both transverse and longitudinal directions. It is possible that the lack of lengthwise rigidity led to the collapse, or at any rate the replacement, of a number of the earliest roof systems, which may explain the existence of so many roofs that are apparently nearly as old as their substructures, but which are not contemporary, like Braxted church.

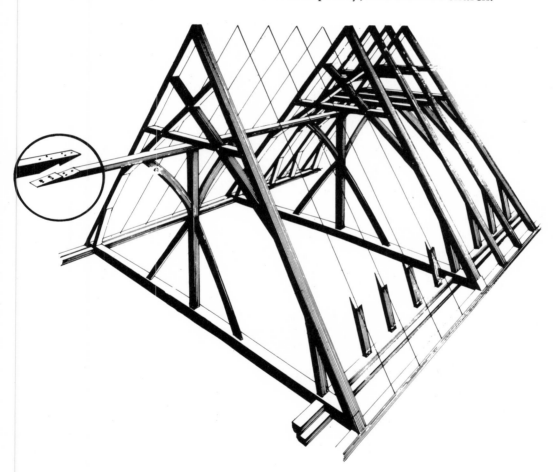

Fig. 9. Part of the nave roof at White Roding

11

The way in which this lengthwise strengthening of scissor-braced roofs was effected is illustrated by the nave roof of a building of Norman style: the church at White Roding. This roof is illustrated in Fig. 9. It is unlikely to be contemporary with the general fabric, yet it must have been built within two centuries of the building's initial completion. It may date from the second half of the 13th century, and the *trait-de-Jupiter* scarf joint, shown on the end of the collar purlin in the drawing, is supporting evidence for this ascription. One and a half bays are illustrated because the roof was repaired at some unknown time when double collars were evidently fashionable, since these were fitted between the older scissored couples. This intrusion should be helpful when a date for the inception of such double collars has to be determined. The roof has double wall plates that are connected only by the tie beams at the juncture of each bay's length.

The main development occurring during this period was a proliferation of scissor-braced roofs, the earliest of which (at Little Coggeshall, *c*. 1220) had secret notched laps, and what appear to be the latest (those over the South Chapel at Great Sampford), had scissor braces like those at Merton College, Oxford, with chase-tenoned end joints, apparently dating from *c*. 1280. Of the several Essex roofs that can be ascribed to this period only the White Roding example is double-framed, with its collar purlin providing for the lengthwise stability of the couples. Equally important was the introduction of the crown post, to carry the collar purlin, and these posts and central purlins will be shown to have become almost invariable in the county later on. During the final decade of the 13th century the use of lap-jointing, either dovetailed or notched, ceased so far as the available evidence indicates; and whilst the use of scissor-bracing continued, the braces were fitted by means of chase tenons. The cross-halved joint needed to effect the crossing of scissors had to be retained for certain purposes; but the most recent scissor braces even dispensed with this halving, as will be shown under the Decorated period.

III

During: The Decorated Period: c. 1250 – c. 1350

It has been stated that the 'architecture of England between 1250 and 1350 was, although the English do not know it, the most forward, the most important, and the most inspired in Europe' (Sir N. Pevsner, 1943, 128). It is to the last 50 years of this period that a high percentage of Essex church carpentry seems to be attributable. Some roofs, including one lean-to aisle example, will be described and illustrated in order to show what changes were occurring in the county during this time. The first example among these is of the least certain date, and has been included because reasons exist — and will be given when the examples are summarised — for a dating not later than the beginning of this period.

The church at Danbury has a very complicated building history. It is covered by a visually complex collection of roofs, at least one of which (that over the nave) was rebuilt after being damaged by a medieval tempest. The Royal Commission stated that the earliest part of the fabric found at the time of their examination was the north aisle, the lower courses of which they ascribed to the 12th century. This was much altered in the latter part of the 13th century. The roof over the aisle today is of the type illustrated in Fig. 10. Its soffit forms an arch composed of four 'compassed' timbers, all of which are chase-tenoned into the rafters and collars; its eastern end is ribbed and panelled, and has carved heads representing kings, and possibly queens, which were applied to the sole pieces early in the 15th century. The remainder of the couples are left exposed, and at the west gable the terminal frame is embedded in the masonry, having every appearance of being contemporary with it. The wall plates which are shown in silhouette at the right of the drawing appear to be later additions to the roof.

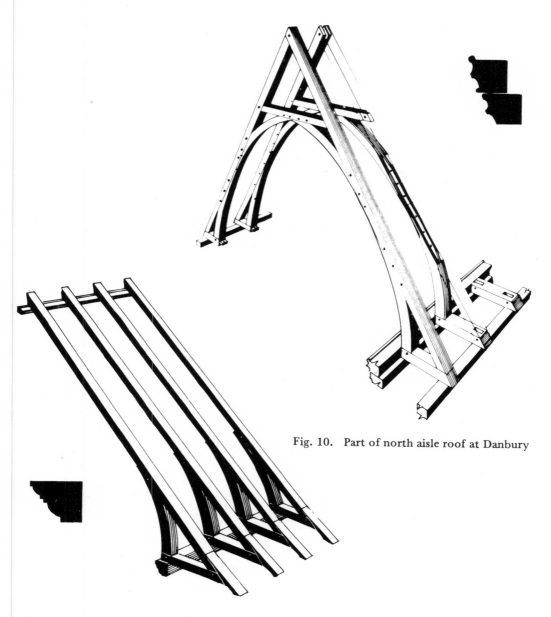

Fig. 10.   Part of north aisle roof at Danbury

Fig. 11.   Part of north aisle roof at Great Sampford

Fig. 11 shows a fraction of the roof over the north aisle at Great Sampford. The greater part of this building is thought to date from the early 14th century, and a recent investigator has ascribed it to no later than *c.* 1320, (Sir N. Pevsner, 1958, 128), a date which applies to both the chancel and aisle, together with its roof. An obvious similarity between this and the preceding specimen is the use of curved, or 'compassed' ashlar pieces, and had this roof not been of a single slope it would have possessed a similarly arched soffit. The section of the single and interior wall plate is shown in silhouette. The church at Foxearth is deceptive in that its Victorian restoration succeeded in making the entire fabric look Victorian, but other extensive structural works were carried out in the middle decade of the 14th century when the north aisle was rebuilt and widened, and the north chapel added. It is to this that the existing nave roof belongs, and this is illustrated in Fig. 12. The principal frames are heavily wall-pieced and collared, with equally strong and diagonally tied arch braces. The curvature of this arching is of the type that became common towards the end of the period. The common rafters are framed into seven cants, and their base triangles are formed by ashlars and soles that are tenoned into a heavy interior wall plate.

Fig. 12.   Nave roof at Foxearth

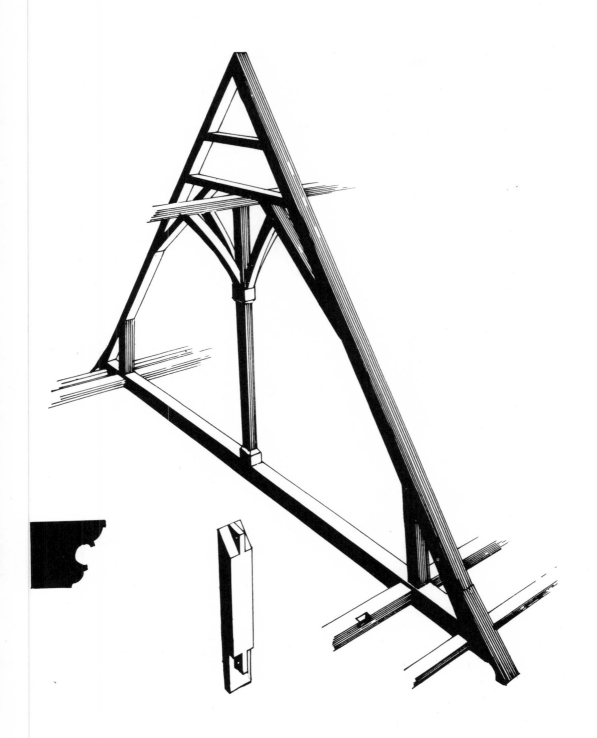

Fig. 13.   Part of nave roof at Hockley

15

The nave roof at Hockley (Fig. 13) rests at its northern wall plate on an arcade ascribed to the 13th century, but the date of the roof itself is uncertain. It has straight and slender tie beams mounting crown posts of archaic type, treated with square capitals and bases; the collars are doubled above the resultant seven cants. The interior wall plate has the deep hollow moulding that was common during the early 14th century. It would seem that plain crown posts such as these that were chamfered, either at their corners or on their flats, to produce a capital and base effect, succeeded the early absolutely plain examples in the nave roof at White Roding, which have already been dealt with.

The nave roof at Pattiswick is illustrated in Figs. 14 and 15, the first showing its western timber-framed gable which now abuts the chancel end, and the central crown-post frame. The second drawing shows the details of this roof, and in particular the treatment of the crown post, the capital of which has a succession of scroll mouldings of a type that was most widely used between c. 1280 and c. 1340. The base has begun to presage the tall spreading form common during the ensuing Perpendicular period. The eaves triangle of this roof is shown at the right of the drawing, and it is unusual in that the ashlars are jointed into the sole pieces.

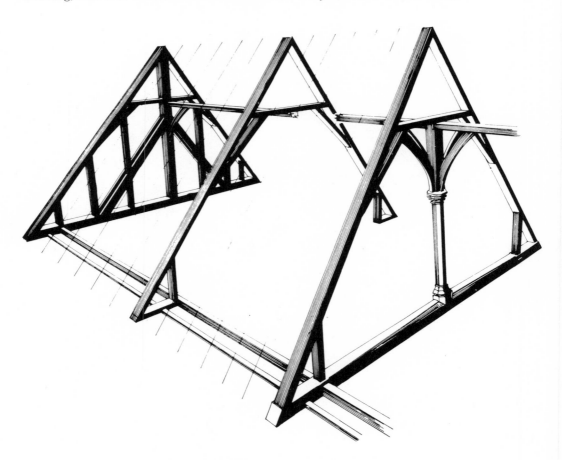

Fig. 14.   Part of nave roof at Pattiswick

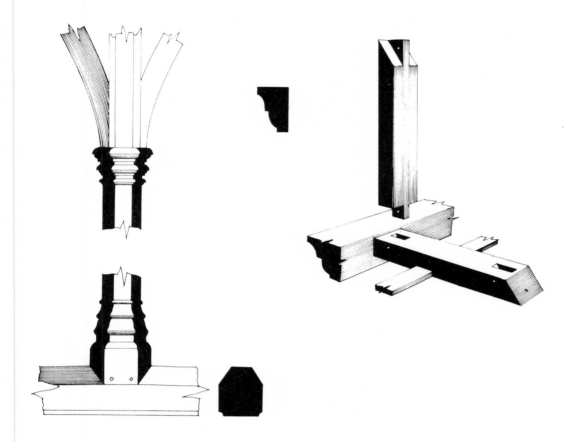

Fig. 15. Pattiswick: showing capital and base treatment of central crown post

The roof illustrated in Fig. 16 is that which covers the nave of Messing church, a structure that can be dated by the heraldic achievement carved on one of its members to sometime between 1344 and 1362, as will be more fully explained in the summary of the period. The frame designed to clear the chancel arch is the single hammer frame at the right of the illustration, while the principal frames defining the bays of the roof are of the type shown centrally in the drawing. These are remarkable in that they present a smoothly-arched soffit that is contrived largely by cutting into the rafters, and by the highly-cambered collars having 'compassed' lower edges. To complete this arch, curved wall pieces are fitted against the ashlars. All the common couples of the two bays which have escaped restoration are in seven cants, like the couple shown to the left of the figure. The profile of the single, heavy, internal wall plate is shown in silhouette at the right-hand edge of the illustration.

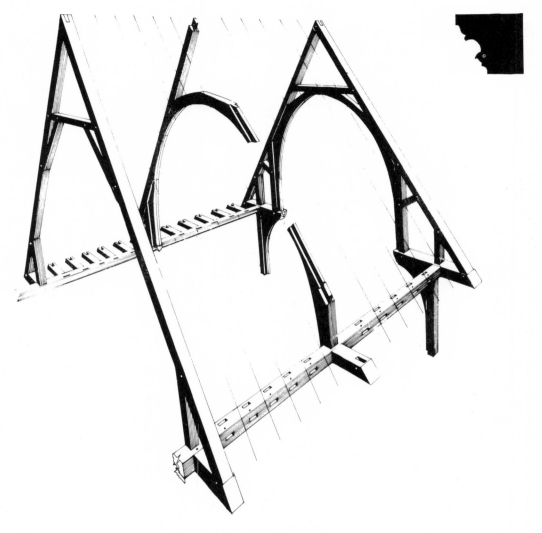

Fig. 16.   Part of nave roof at Messing

The nave roof of Eastwood church is another example of the crown-post category that admits of a very early ascription, and is illustrated in Fig. 17, together with its most significant structural and decorative details. The tie beams are straight and mount octagonal crown posts that have scroll-type mouldings at their capitals; the collar purlin is scarfed with the stop-splayed variety of scarf joint, and the eaves triangulation is contrived in the remarkable manner previously noted in respect of the Hockley roof. This last detail is shown at the lower right corner of the drawing.

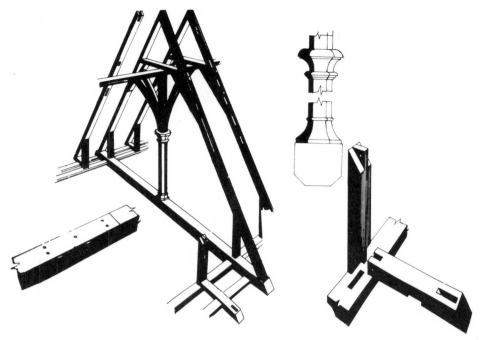

Fig. 17. Nave roof at Eastwood

'The half century from 1285 to 1335 witnessed the most brilliant display of sheer inventiveness in the whole history of English medieval architecture.' (Kidson, 1965, 106.) This inventiveness was not reflected in the works of the Essex roof-carpenters during the period, and the examples described are but the logical continuation of earlier methods. The rare and entirely arched roof over the north aisle at Danbury, with which the nine 'Decorated' examples were introduced, represents a type that is widespread in Germany and can be found at the churches of Mittelzell, Walberberg, Quedlinburg and Münzenberg, to name but four of many, none of which is dated later than the 13th century (Reuter). The portraits carved and painted on the extended eastern sole pieces, the crenellated wall plates and probably the ribbed and panelled soffit date from the first quarter of the 15th century, as one of the ladies' head-dresses indicates. These parts were added, however, to the soffit of the earlier roof, which is pegged through its edges in the normal manner, and through its faces in a manner that doubtless derives from the more ancient butt-notched roof at Ongar. This construction would therefore date from the same building operation as does the existing late 13th-century north aisle (c. 1300, as suggested by the investigators of the Royal Commission). The lean-to roof existing at Great Sampford, again over the north aisle, is an example of exactly the same principle applied to a different situation, and this example is dated to c. 1320. This roof type has been likened to the canvas tilt that was carried on hoops to cover a wagon, hence the term 'wagon roof'.

The introduction of double framing into roofing, exemplified by the nave roof at White Roding *c*. 1260, indicates that the 'trussed rafter' formation, presenting a soffit of seven canted planes (probably introduced in the form it has over the chancel at Ongar), had become inextricably involved with the crown-post system, which employed this form for all its common-rafter couples. The theory that 'trussed' rafters (as the seven-canted type has long been named, in error, since it is not trussed at all) may have derived from scissored roofs after *c*. 1300, as a result of omitting the scissors' ends from above the collars, cannot be reconciled with this evidence. It is more probable that these 'trussed' rafters, which most commonly had chase-tenoned joints, evolved from the butt-notched type used at Ongar at the end of the 11th century; and, having achieved by the use of lap-jointing a capability for resisting their own outward spread, they were very widely used, since they needed few obstructing tie beams. Examples of the two systems—crown post with collar purlin, and seven-canted rafter roofs—survive in similar numbers: the author found 65 of the former, and 76 of the latter. It has long been generally admitted that the seven-canted roofs are virtually undatable, since they do not usually incorporate any decorative features; and it is suggested that many date from this period and are coeval with the earliest crown-post roofs, thus numbering among the oldest surviving types.

On this evidence it seems that the type of roof that had arches from wall piece to collar was a separate development, although an example with scissor braces that are arched thus to their intersection is known in Suffolk (Sir N. Pevsner, 1961, 128). This type of roof maintained the tradition of single framing for a long time, and was further developed during the ensuing Perpendicular period; but it represents a minority of the surviving historic examples, a fact which emphasizes its lack of stability and durability. The next two crown-post systems illustrate the earlier type of such roofs to be found among the 65 examined, and indicate either the beginning of a wide usage of double collars, or the continuing advocation of this principle by a minority of craftsmen since the time of the roof at Waltham Abbey.

Another type of roof that may have continued from early times, Ongar chancel, and Mittelzell—but in a minority—is that with its timbers forming an arched underside, as also do the principal-frames of the nave-roof at Messing, shown in Fig. 16. As has been stated, one of the ashlar pieces at Messing is carved with an heraldic achievement, the arms of the Baynard family, who held the manor of Messing from as early as *c*. 1272. The escutcheon, which is of 14th-century shape, bears a label of five points, the first of the heraldic marks of cadence, and one which indicates that the bearer of the arms is an eldest son. The only Baynard likely to have been the bearer of these arms (and therefore responsible for this roof) would have been the third Thomas Baynard, who would have borne the label on his arms between 1344 and 1362. It is within this period that the Messing roof must have been built, and the profile of the wall plate confirms such a dating.

The Eastwood roof, which embodies an early crown post, serves to emphasize the fact that tie beams continued to be straight during these years, and that ashlar pieces were strongly jointed into the wall plates in order to enhance the lengthwise stability of the couples, as did the collar purlin.

During the Perpendicular Period: c. 1350–c. 1450,
and the Tudor Period; c. 1450–c.1550

The nave at St. Peter's, Goldhanger, has a crown-post roof with three tie beams that are mounted on wall pieces with traceried spandrels, and mouldings of unusual interest. Perhaps the most remarkable feature is the chamfering of every constituent timber of the roof, including the smallest and least important. This roof is shown in Fig. 18, in which sections of the crown posts, wall pieces and the composite tie beams are also given. The date for this example should be in the second quarter of the 14th century. A very different roof which could, apparently, date from the same period is the roof over the nave at High Roding, which is illustrated with wall-plate sections in Fig. 19. It is a roof with double collars to every couple, and framed into a seven-cant underside, there being three bays of only four rafter couples each. The section of the wall plate, which is shown at the left of the drawing, is difficult to date and is unique in Essex. The working of the small bead or bowtell inside the three-quarter-circle hollow moulding seems to presage the arrival of the later beaded casement. The external wall plates have been renewed, as is shown by their scarfing. This can be seen from the churchyard, and is of the edge-halved and bridle-butted type.

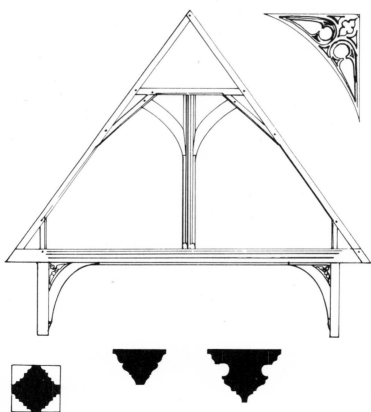

Fig. 18.   Part of nave roof at Goldhanger

Fig. 19. Part of nave roof at High Roding

The roof over the nave of Doddinghurst is another example that cannot be dated at all, since it embodies no acceptable criteria for that purpose. The hollow moulding on the wall plates is not peculiar to any period, and the quadrate section of the crown post was common to several periods; but the existence of the ridge piece mounted on king pieces and alternate double collars tends to preclude any late date ascriptions. The carcase of the nave is composed of flint-rubble and pebbles, but the south door has dog-tooth ornament and is attributed to the 13th century. The roof, which is illustrated in Fig. 20, could well date from the early 14th century in view of the experimental nature of its construction. The ridge piece, in its diagonal position, is unique in the county among surviving crown-post roofs.

The church of All Saints at Dovercourt has what is essentially a Norman nave. This is covered by a roof that is evidently Perpendicular, as the style of its crown posts' feet and capitals testifies, and the beginning of the 15th century seems a possible ascription. At the half-bay intervals this roof is fitted with double collars so closely spaced that they clasp the collar purlin, a feature that otherwise only occurs at Fingringhoe. This roof is illustrated in Fig. 21, with the details of its wall plate and sections inset. The braces beneath the tie beams' ends must be fitted into wall pieces, but the thickness of the rendering and plaster on the interior of the walls is so great that these timbers can no longer be seen.

22

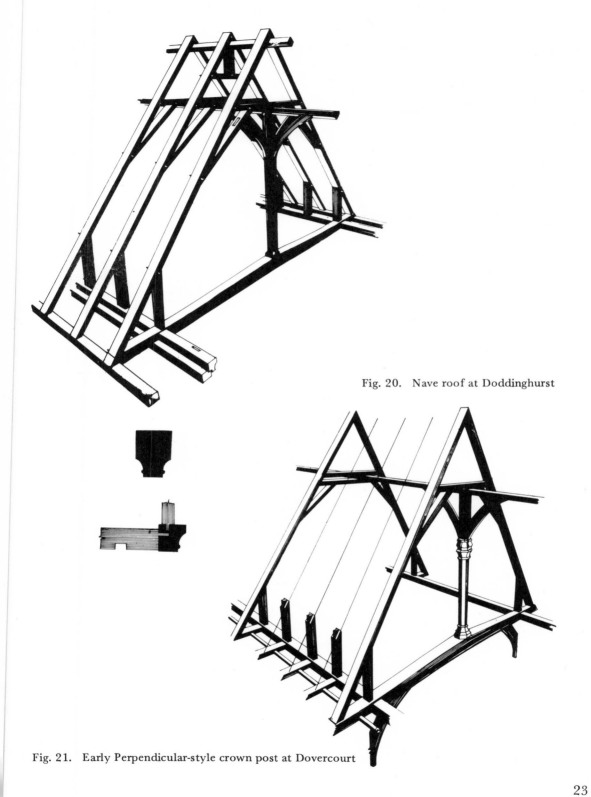

Fig. 20.   Nave roof at Doddinghurst

Fig. 21.   Early Perpendicular-style crown post at Dovercourt

The central frame of the nave roof covering the small, 13th-century church of Ulting is a timber arch built in four compassed pieces. This is illustrated in Fig. 22, with the section of its wall pieces and wall plates inset. The two bays of the roof are short and comprise four couples each: they are framed into seven cants, and the wall plates are crested with the 'billet' type of crenellation that was for a long period universal.

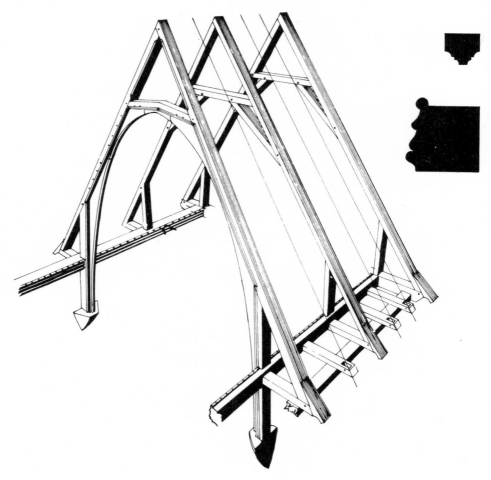

Fig. 22.   Part of nave roof at Ulting

One of the most important roofs in the county is shown in Plate II: it has a ceiling of plaster and cannot, consequently, be examined or drawn. This very impressive roof, which covers the nave of the church of St. Ouen, at Fingringhoe, is of a structural design that probably derives from the roof at Foxearth, and of which only two examples have survived. It is arched to its collars, which are doubled and clasp the purlin at each half-bay juncture, and is fitted with diagonal spurs that embrace the arch timbers, which are cut from a single piece. The inner ends of the diagonal spurs are carved with great sensitivity and skill into a series of eight portraits, which

24

are the only seriously studied, and evidently accurate, portraits in the county (except for those in stone). (See Plate II.) A great deal of information concerning these details is published in the *Guide for Visitors* (R. Boustred & K. Trace, 1969), and two of them represent John Doreward, once Speaker of the House of Commons, and his wife Isabella. Doreward, who is second from the left in the top row in Plate III, was granted the manor of Fingringhoe in 1401, and on his death in 1420 it passed to his widow, who is at the extreme left in the top row of Plate III. Isabella Doreward died in 1426, and the manor then passed by royal grant to the Archbishop of Canterbury, Henry Chichele. The headdress Isabella is wearing in the portrait is of the type known as 'nebule', and it can be dated to the closing decades of the 14th century. The dating of this roof is greatly assisted by the portraits, and despite the uncertain identity of their subjects, the two women's headdresses do positively indicate a date early in the 15th century; any date soon after 1401, the year the Dorewards acquired the manor, would therefore be reasonable.

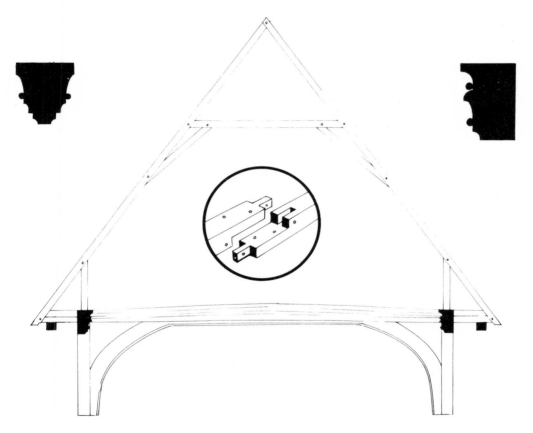

Fig. 23. Part of chancel roof at High Roding

During the first half of the 15th century some tied roofs were apparently built that were framed into seven cants above the beams, with those beams wall-pieced and arch-braced, as in Fig. 23. This degree of elaboration is difficult to explain, since the provision of wall pieces was normally confined to tie beams that were thought likely to sag because they were subjected to weight transmitted through some vertical member, such as a crown post. The sections of the wall plates and wall pieces are illustrated, the former showing the beaked half-roll moulding, which indicates a date early in the century. The roof in question is that over the chancel at High Roding, which is built in two bays, and has this frame at its centre. External wall plates were inserted all round the eaves of this building, and these are scarfed with the edge-halved and bridle-butted joint that was used after c. 1375.

St. Mary's church at Little Burstead has a nave roof that is supported by a single crown-post frame, which is illustrated in Fig. 24; the sections of its various members are included at the edges of the drawing. The direct relationship between the casement and bowtell mouldings on the tie beam, wall piece and inner wall plates indicates that the roof is of a single design, and that it was probably executed with the same tools during the second quarter of the 15th century.

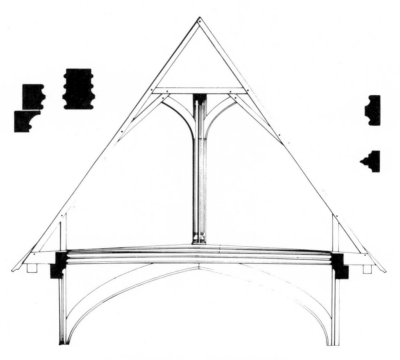

Fig. 24.   Part of nave roof at Little Burstead

The next roof which is shown, in Fig. 25, is that over the nave of Gosfield church, dedicated to St. Katherine, and datable with tolerable certainty by the known facts concerning one of the principal benefactors of this parish. The nave and east window of the existing building are what survives of the church built by Sir Thomas Rolf in 1435, and it is logical to ascribe the roof to this date. The nave is both high and wide, and the construction of this finely executed roof, which is single-framed and arched to its collars, must have been an erection task of complexity and difficulty.

The arch timbers are composite, and their lower pieces approximate to eaves blades since they contain the eaves angle. The collars have clasping ends to hold the principal rafters, and similarly the spur ties clasp the eaves pieces of the arch timbers; the common couples are framed in seven cants.

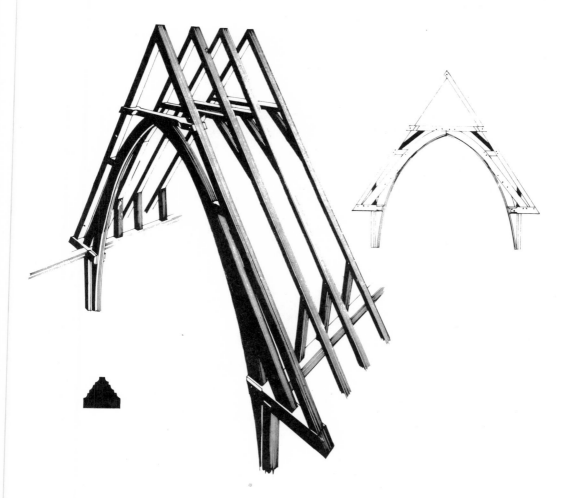

Fig. 25. Nave roof at Gosfield

The nave roof of the church at Middleton, which is dedicated to All Saints, is a curious hybrid of other roof-types that were previously distinct and used singly. It has raised tie beams that tenon into the principals, as do the wall pieces that rise from timber corbels, and there are tracery-pierced spandrels to the arch braces that unite these two members. This roof is illustrated in Fig. 26, as are the tracery designs of the wall-piece spandrels, and the cross sections of the composite inner wall plates.

27

The profile of the inner wall plates indicates a date during the first quarter of the 15th century. There is a ridge piece, diagonally set, which is supported by short king pieces that rise from collars at the bay intervals, and these are braced as shown in the drawing. Finally, the roof has side purlins, upon which the four common rafters of each bay are laid. The corbels and the wall plates both have crenellated crestings.

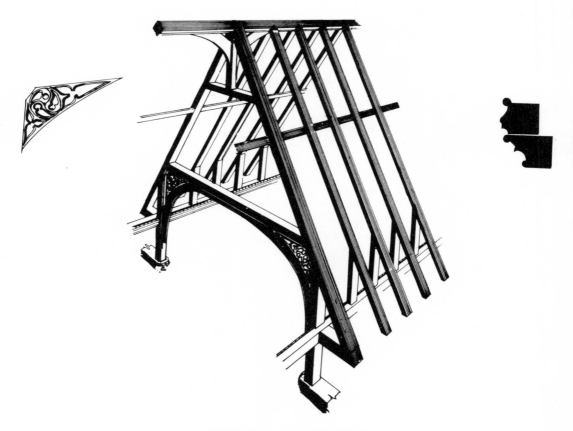

Fig. 26. Nave roof at Middleton

A preoccupation with heavy arch timbers that rise to the collars is again evident in the nave roof at Cressing, which is shown in Fig. 27. Combining as it does structural elements from several different categories of roof, this is another example of carpentry that may have a very wide significance. The specification is a roof in three bays with tie beams on arch-braced wall pieces, arched to its collars, with side purlins and crown pieces with collar purlin engaging high collars, the common couples framed into seven cants. The timber arches below the collars are tied to the principal-rafters by three short timbers, and there are pierced tracery panels between them and the main timbers. Information on one other roof that combines side purlins with collar purlin has been published previously (Hewett, 1969, 119-121), and both this and Cressing date from the first half of the 15th century.

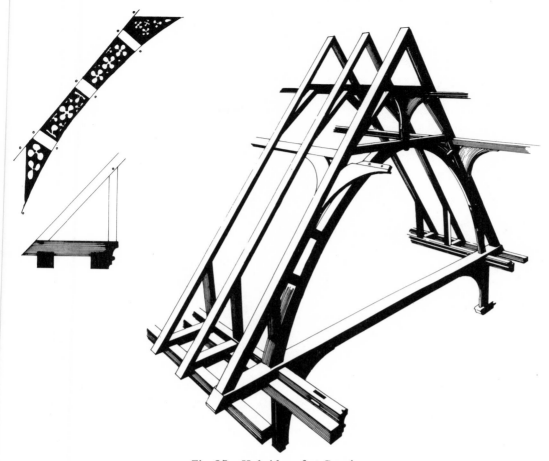

Fig. 27. Hybrid roof at Cressing

Over the nave at Margaretting there is a roof similar to that at Cressing, but it is more ambitious in that it was not fitted with tie beams (Fig. 28). The principal frames are arched to their collars, above which short crown pieces carry a collar purlin; on this rest the high collars of the common rafters, the latter being framed into seven cants. The whole is beautifully cut, and probably dates from the middle years of the 15th century. The main transverse frames are of a type that occurred in at least two others churches in Essex, Orsett and at Fobbing, where they were used as terminal frames.

The nave of Birdbrook church, which is dedicated to St. Augustine of Canterbury, has an evidently early—and at the latest, Norman—carcase, which is spanned by the unique roof illustrated in Fig. 29. It is double-framed by means of butted side purlins, and has six common couples in each bay. This roof is not of the variety termed 'arched-to-collar', or collar-arched, and it is actually eaves-bladed, since the angle of the eaves is held stable by a single grown bend of timber that forms both wall piece and rafter brace: the resulting shape is not an arch. The internal wall plate has crenellated decoration, as have the collars, and (as shown in the insets) the mouldings on both combine ogees and hollows, which must date from the first half of the 15th century. In this example the common rafters are laid on the outer faces of the purlins and the ridge piece, and tenon into the sole pieces.

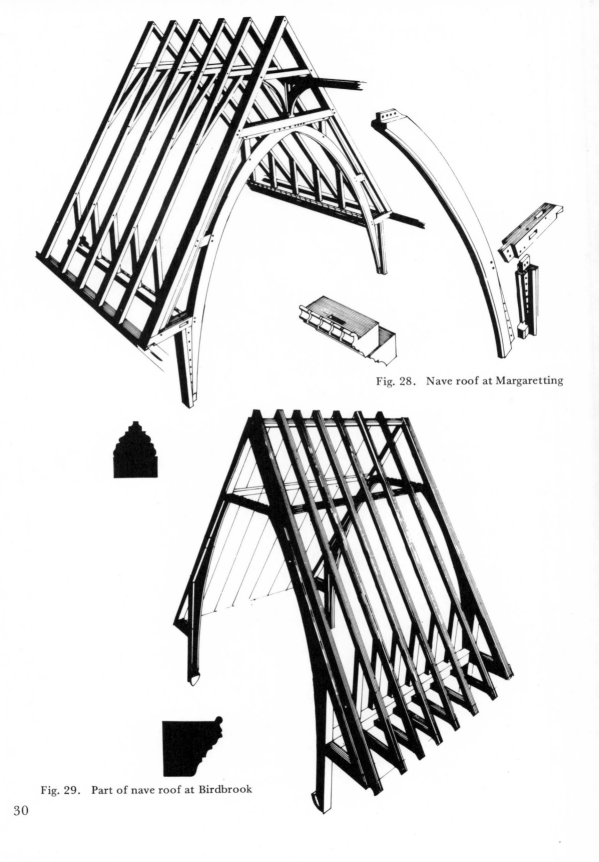

Fig. 28. Nave roof at Margaretting

Fig. 29. Part of nave roof at Birdbrook

30

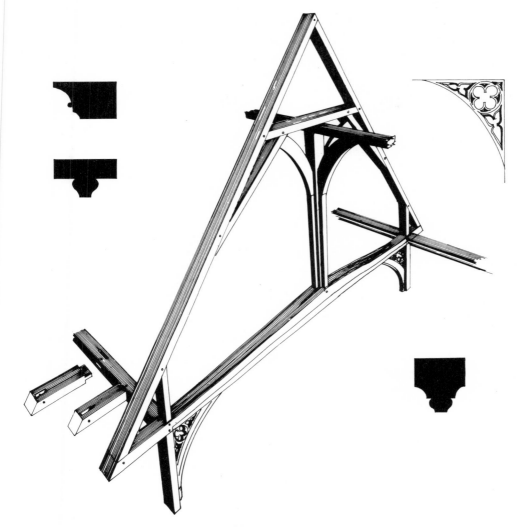

Fig. 30.   Part of nave roof at Chipping Ongar

Ridgewell has a clerestory roof that is well arched to its collars from canopied wall pieces that have been defaced. The arches are built in four timbers, and the invariable weakness of this method is shown in Plate IV, in which the blacksmith's repairs can be seen at the upper left, beneath one purlin. The frames at the half-bay points formerly had angels or some similar device affixed to their projecting sole pieces, which have also been removed. The roof probably dates from the first half of the 15th century and has a spiral leaf ornament carved along its wall plates. A crown-post roof that may be contemporary or mid-15th-century is the nave roof at Chipping Ongar, which is illustrated in Fig. 30 with its moulding profiles inset. The crown-post roof continued to be constructed in this direct manner with only single collars for some time, and usually, as in this example, with a single wall plate. I am advised that the section of the wall pieces shown at the lower right of the drawing includes a 15th-century version of the roll-and-fillet moulding (Forrester, 1972).

A new type of roof seems to have appeared at Stebbing. There it covers the chancel, which is dated like the whole fabric of the church to *c.* 1360, or perhaps a little earlier (authorities are not fully agreed). It is a roof of *six* cants, arched to the collars and with tracery (mainly quatrefoiled) in the spandrels formed by the collar braces. Similar roofs exist at Liston and Bulmer, both over the chancels. The Stebbing example is panelled between its grooved rafters, as a result of which its construction cannot be properly examined. This roof is illustrated in Plate V. All three examples of the panelled and six-canted roof seem to date from the last quarter of the 15th century in so far as they relate to the fenestration of the chancels they cover.

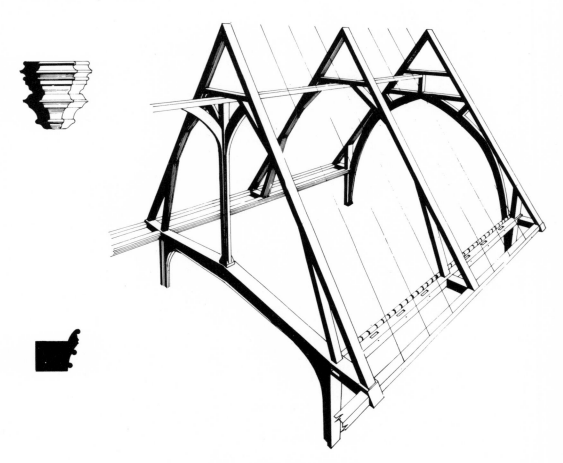

Fig. 31. Nave roof at Panfield

Some flat-pitched tie-beam roofs, with wall pieces and arch braces, were built during the 15th century; probably during the middle decades, as is apparently the case with the fine nave roof at Kelvedon, shown in Plate VI. This has recently been restored. The ridge piece is supported by obtuse arches, built in three timbers from the tie beams; imitation hammerbeams carved with various figures are

32

provided at the half-bay intervals. The stone corbels beneath the wall pieces are semi-octagonal, and these confirm a mid-century ascription for the roof. Also mid-15th-century but lacking any Tudor styling is the roof over the nave at St. Mary's church, Panfield, illustrated in Fig. 31. At the centre this has a crown post of the cross-quadrate section with four braces; the seven common rafters in each bay are framed into seven cants, and at the chancel arch there is a decadent and structurally weak arch from wall pieces to collar. This arch is diagonally and compressively strutted near its top, and the whole frame is visually most unsatisfactory. All the ashlar pieces are long and inclined, and the tie beam is wall-pieced with knees in the angles.

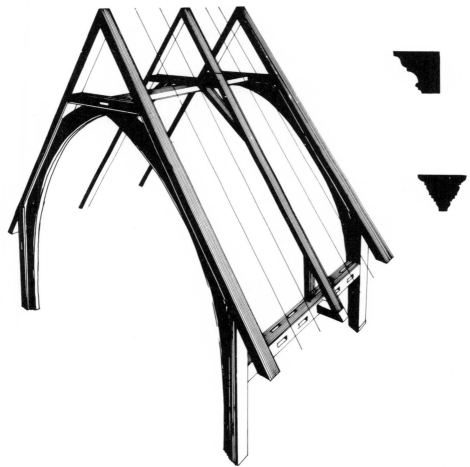

Fig. 32. Part of nave roof at Great Horkesley

The main roof at Great Horkesley church, dedicated to All Saints, is one of the most satisfying 15th-century roofs in the county. It is framed in two bays, one of which is shown in Fig. 32, each bay having five common rafters that are framed into seven cants. The sections of the heavy wall plate and of the deep wall pieces are both shown at the right of the drawing, and the collar purlin in this roof is tenoned

33

into the principal-collars, as the drawing indicates. Great Henny church, which is dedicated to St. Mary, has a nave roof with alternate tie beams, and collar-arched frames. The tie beams are wall-pieced and have four-centred arch braces; they mount queen posts which tenon into the rafters, and are arch-braced to the collars. The whole roof has side purlins that are wind-braced, as shown at the side of Fig. 33.

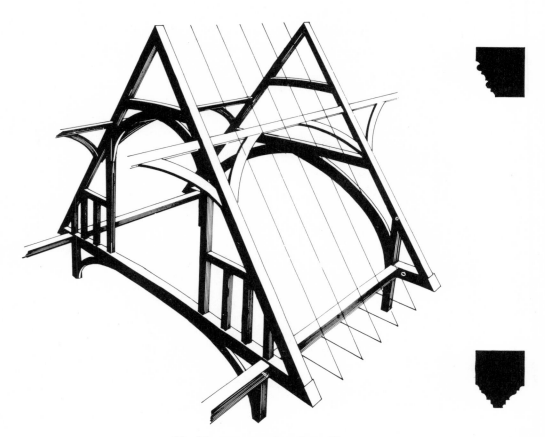

Fig. 33. Nave roof at Great Henny

An unusually obtusely pitched roof that is arch-braced to the collars, in a rather weak manner, is that over the chancel at West Mersea. This is shown in Fig. 34, with the sections of its wall plates and wall pieces, inset. This example, according to the sections planed on its members, dates from the third quarter of the 15th century. It is a well-wrought specimen, but one which has not jointed the two arch timbers strongly at their apexes, as a result of which its survival is surprising. An uncommonly rich decorated flat roof that was built for a south aisle is that at Steeple Bumpstead, which is shown in Plate VII, whose date is uncertain but is either early, or mid-, 15th century. The foliate motifs are all good and well-cut, and the cabled decoration to the arched members is rare and visually satisfying.

34

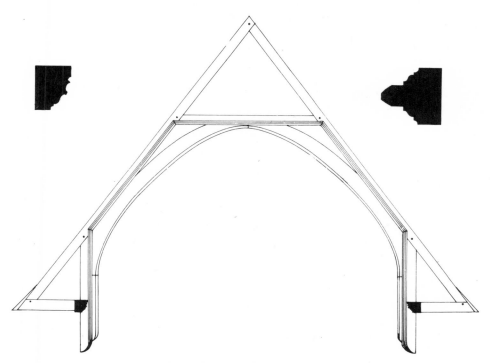

Fig. 34.   Part of chancel roof at West Mersea

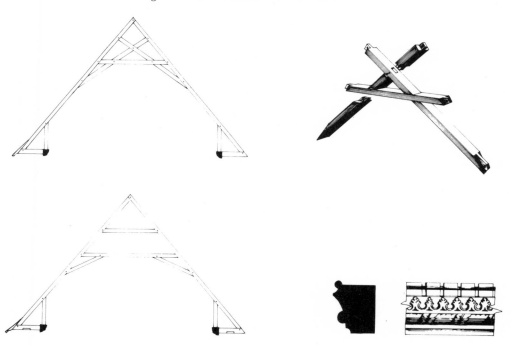

Fig. 35.   Belchamp St. Paul's: showing aspects of roof construction

Roofing in six cants, as a development from the preceding and invariable seven cants, seems to have been introduced during the final decades of the 15th century; and the chancel roof at Ramsey, which seems to date from the very opening of the 16th century, resolves this development by comprising exactly five cants.

The north chapel of St. Michael and All Angels at Berechurch is covered by the impressive hammerbeam roof illustrated in Plate VIII. All the timbers are richly decorated, mainly with foliage motifs, the shields that have been added to the inner ends of the hammers are rococo and stylistically a little incongruous. The date ascribed for this church is *c.* 1500. The section of the porch and chancel wall plates at St. Andrew's, Belchamp St. Paul, is given at the lower right-hand corner of Fig. 35; the motif introduced above the roll-moulding which is carved with a spirally-wound vine leaf does not appear before this example, and evidently derives from the 'honeysuckle scroll' of antiquity which can be seen, for example, upon the Lysicrates monument at Athens, dated 335 B.C. (Bannister Fletcher, *A History of Architecture*, 1956, 111.) This motif came into wide use on oriel windowsills as a relief, and as a cresting on timbers like purlins, or wall plates. The actual framing of this chancel roof is in seven cants with double collars.

The nave roof is important, being the type derived from Salisbury Cathedral's north-east transept of *c.* 1237. (Hewett, 1980, Fig. 91, p. 105.) These were formed of five short lengths and acted in compression; the Belchamp examples are illustrated at the top right of Fig. 35. Such frames can easily be confused with the real scissor-braced examples, and to avoid mistakes the edge-pegs must be counted.

Gestingthorpe has a nave roof with double hammerbeams, the hammer posts are mortised over the beams and, as a result, are finished as pendants in both tiers — these may be seen clearly in Plate IX. The tracery panels fitted between the principal rafters and the backs of the hammer posts are richly varied; two inscriptions have been found in these areas, of which that on the north side reads: 'Peter Baynard & Marget hys wyf', and that on the south: 'Thomas Loveda & Alys hys wyf'. Both families were residents of this parish from early times, and they jointly donated this magnificent roof to the church, *c.* 1500 it is thought.

Another roof of this date, or of the opening decades of the 16th century, is that above the chancel of St. Nicholas' church at Laindon, framed in seven cants. This is a fine example enriched with Tudor-rose reliefs as well as with tracery, crenellations, and on its wall plates, the 'Honeysuckle' cresting noted at Belchamp St. Paul's. (See Plate X.) This is an important roof, insofar as it affects the evolutionary sequence: it has arch-braced collars, side purlins *and* a collar purlin. It is also grooved on each timber for the panelling between rafters.

A curious roof that is also attributable to the opening decades of the 16th century is that shown in Plate XI. This covers the chancel at Little Hallingbury church. It has three main frames with single hammerbeams, and the common couples between them are braced to their collars with thin timbers forming depressed arches, above the apexes of which the collars are weakly cranked. This is an example of structural decadence, since cranked collars are less able than straight ones to resist either compression or extension. The wall plates are carved with vine-leaf trails, which wind spirally round a roll moulding.

36

Saffron Walden has one of the largest churches in this county, and one that is rich in works of fine carpentry—all Perpendicular—as is the finish of the greater part of the fabric. For the present purpose only two of the various roofs will be mentioned, those above the nave and the chancel. There is little certainty as to the dates of either of these, but there are good grounds for believing that the nave roof, shown in Plate XII, must date from c. 1520, since the nave clerestory is known to have been rebuilt at this time. This is a magnificent roof, camber-beamed at each bay and half-bay interval; the bay beams are wall-pieced semi-octagonally, and from these pieces four-centred arch braces rise to the beams and to the wall plates in such a manner as fits them closely over the rear arches of the clerestory lights. All the resultant spandrels are filled with timber tracery, and the arch timbers are carved with a flattened, zig-zag, version of the vine-leaf trail. The straight timbers, including the common rafters, are all roll-moulded, in groupings which typify the first quarter of the 16th century.

The chancel at Saffron Walden has a similar roof, with numerous bays of three common rafters each, four-centred arches beneath camber beams with traceried spandrels, and pendants at their centres—as is illustrated in Plate XIII. This may date from the last quarter of the 15th century, so far as documentary evidence goes, and the arch-brace timbers are carved with a form of nebule pattern not noticed elsewhere.

Layer Marney's church was rebuilt by the first Lord Marney between 1505 and 1520 (Pevsner, 1954, 237) and to this rebuilding the roof over its chancel, logically, would belong. (See Fig. 36.) This is a curious example that has both common collars and side purlins, inclined ashlar pieces like those in very early roofs, and, most unusual of all, windbraces rising from the side purlins to the principal rafters, at their apex ends. It is a good roof, well wrought, but over elaborate. An aisle roof that is included solely for its excellence is that shown in Plate XIV. It covers the north aisle of the church of St. Mary in Bocking. The frame of this is very simple, but the fitting of all the joints and the execution of the mouldings is of the highest quality. It is interesting to see the two forms of the vine-leaf decoration in this example: the leaf is cut as spiral on the central principal which has a knee and a wall piece, and as a flattened zig-zag in the other cases. The jointing of the wall plates into the edges of the principals is cunningly contrived, and is well worth a detailed examination, as are the elaborate bosses at the central crossings.

The church of St. Nicholas at Castle Hedingham has one of the most impressive large roofs in this county, double-hammerbeam, traceried and richly accoutred with pendants. This is illustrated in Plate XV. A village tradition alleges that the carpenter was local and named Thomas Loveday—one of the names inscribed on the similar roof at Gestingthorpe. A reasonable date for this work and for the style of its decorative carvings would be the first quarter of the 16th century and, if it is relevant, 'Thomas Loveda's' will was proved in 1535. The leaf-trail motif is present on both hammerbeams and wall plates but upon close inspection it bears little resemblance to earlier examples of the kind. Iron tie rods have been introduced here, as was evidently necessary, and they serve to underline the inherent weakness of this category of roof framing—which constitutes a weakened form of secondary raftering.

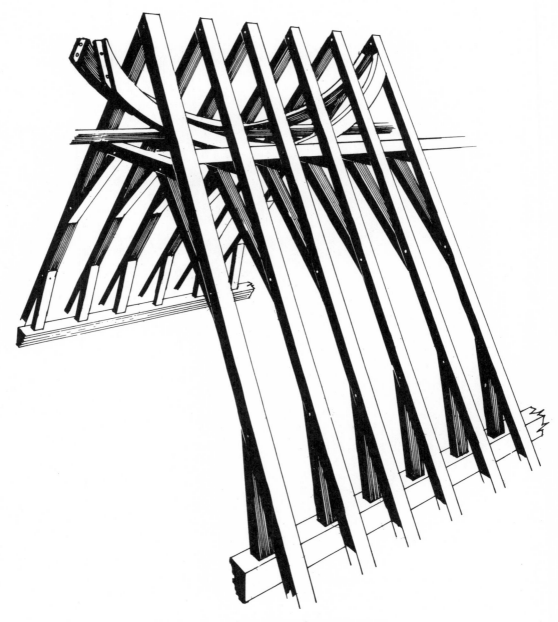

Fig. 36. Part of chancel roof at Layer Marney

Of a date within the first half of this century is the huge, depressed-ridged, and short queen-posted roof over the nave clerestory at High Easter — the church of St. Mary the Virgin. This is shown in Plate XVI, in which it can be seen that both the tracery and the leaf-trail decorations have almost forgotten their origins. This roof, like that at Saffron Walden, has side arcading of planks over the clerestory lights, and carvings of great interest occur at the purlin and rafter crossings.

The architecture of the long period between *c.* 1350 and the Reformation was usually described as Perpendicular, but this has been altered by Dr. J. H. Harvey's definitive work, *The Perpendicular Style* (1978), wherein the time-span is divided into Perpendicular, 1330-1485, and Tudor from *c.* 1450-1550. For the present purpose works covering the entire period have been left in their original grouping because certain specific developments in carpentry have been shown (C. A. Hewett, 1980, 203) to extend, without interruption, from the first into the second phase of style. It has been considered that carpentry became more ambitious during this period (P. Kidson, 1965, 106), but this is a view about which numerous reservations must be made; adherence to the visual style and to its decorative detail frequently induced craftsmen of a high order of skill to abandon structural soundness in favour of conformity to the national taste. One of the most striking effects of the style was its advocation of low-pitched roofs, termed 'camberbeam roofs', and exemplified by those at Saffron Walden; this choice effectively reduced the roof to a floor. Furthermore, treatment of floor soffits, as timber ceilings that equally expressed the style, reduced the structural soundness of floors, their nadir being reached in Morton's Tower at Lambeth Palace in *c.* 1490 (C. A. Hewett, 1980, 227).

Among the examples described, that shown in Fig. 18, from over the nave at Goldhanger, is perhaps more Decorated in character than Perpendicular, and many roofs that continued to use steep pitches can only be ascribed to the style of the Perpendicular by reference to moulding profiles. This is true of the nave roof at High Roding, where a bowtell—or roll—was fitted inside a three-quarter circle hollow, apparently presaging the beaded casement that was to be most favoured during the period. The crown-post roof was used throughout this period, but not to the exclusion of types like the Ulting example in Fig. 22, which is arched to the collar, centrally; nor the tie-beamed chancel roof at High Roding with its wall pieces and arch braces, beneath couples of seven cants—an example that seems to lack any sound basis of tradition.

The next roof, which is shown in Fig. 24 and taken from the nave at Little Burstead, is another good example of a roof built absolutely traditionally and soundly, but styled, so far as its decorative treatment is concerned, in the manner of this period—with arch braces of depressed, four-centred curvature. This is not a Perpendicular roof, but merely the application of Perpendicular styling to a type of framing that could otherwise convincingly typify earlier periods. The ambitions which have been attributed to carpenters of this period are expressed in the rather varied roofs that follow: those at Gosfield, Middleton, Cressing, and Margaretting (Figs. 25-28 inclusive). It is not true in these cases that a desire to span greater widths of nave than had previously been customary gave rise to the inventive approach they indicate; they express convictions on the part of their makers that the wide range of proven methods for building stable pitched roofs, which had been tried until the opening half of the 15th century, could, and probably should, be combinable into something novel and perhaps superior.

The roof, which was stabilised by resting on its timber arch (like that at Gosfield), needed some huge grown bends before its wide span across that church became possible. It does not constitute a technical development so much as a superlative exposition of a type of framing that had for long been developing. The Middleton roof is one of the combinations of plural principles: it is experimental, visually, and not of any peculiar merit—not one of the more successful hybrids of this period. The Cressing roof, shown in Fig. 27, is visually a more successful hybrid of types, and a greater number of them are combined (four categories): crown post with collar purlin, principal rafter with side purlins, arched bracing to collars, and tie beams with wall pieces and arch braces. This carpenter, it seems, had no more faith in any one of these systems than the others. These few combinations of roof frames culminate in the nave roof at Margaretting, which is shown in Fig. 28. This is relatively simple and combines only two systems, crown pieces and collar purlin, with arch-braced collars and spur ties, the result being a visually impressive and well-framed roof.

An innovation in roofing, that was evidently a successful one and probably peculiar to the first half of the 15th century, is the example shown in Fig. 29, which is one bay of the nave roof at Birdbrook. This is a development of the system which sought to stabilise the roof by resting it upon a timber arch; in this case the arch was truncated and left only the two timber arcs, that contained the angles formed by the roof pitches, and the vertical walls—the eaves. It is, therefore, an eaves-bladed roof; this was a system that derived from cruck blades, which was rather widely used at this time for the eaves angles of brick houses that had timber roofs. The Ridgewell roof, which is illustrated in Plate IV, is a development of the arch-braced collar and wall-pieced roof; it is very finely wrought and was formerly even more richly ornate than now. The lowering of the pitch of this roof has subjected its arched members to a severe, stretching strain, and the whole frame is beginning to spread dangerously. As the finest example of its kind this specimen will, it is hoped, be reinforced by the most sensitive methods.

Roofs continued to be built in the firmly established crown-post tradition, but the adoption of octagonal cross sections is marked during the period, and these facilitated the cutting of the characteristically Perpendicular bell spread bases such as shown in Fig. 21, from Dovercourt. The cross, or cross-quadrate section, also continued in use and was modified to express the taste for attached shafts, their arms being cut into various profiles such as 'inverted waves' and drooping off-sets at each reduction of volume. The best example of such existing crown posts is over the north aisle at Stock Harvard. The roof shown in Fig. 32, which is from the nave at Great Horkesley church, is the example that culminates a development which can be followed through Margaretting and earlier specimens, and which aimed at a double-framed roof that was arched to its collars. An example that achieved striking similarity, insofar as the plastered underside allows it to be seen, was the earlier roof at Fingringhoe, but it is unlikely that both used butted collar purlins, as in this example. Examples of depressed and inefficient collar arches continued to be built (as in Figs. 33 and 34) and, in such cases as have survived, their survival is evidently due, in the main, to the thickness and stability of the masonry supporting walls.

The compressive type of scissor bracing, such as is noted under Belchamp St. Paul's, had originated at Salisbury Cathedral, where the surviving roof over the north-east transept, which was completed by c. 1237, constitutes the first recorded example of the type. Fig. 36 shows a bay of the roof over the chancel at Layer

Marney which was apparently built for Lord Marney in c. 1520. This is one of three roofs that were fitted with both side purlins and common collars; in addition this one has wind bracing above the purlins instead of below, as was usual. It has been shown by Mr. L. S. Colchester that these inverted wind braces derived from the inverted arches built into the crossing tower of Wells Cathedral in 1338; and among the various roofs at Wells illustrating this point is that above the Vicars' Exchequer (C. A. Hewett, 1980, 167). The most satisfactory example of this combination is that covering two bays of the nave at Little Braxted, which has bracing of normal curvature placed beneath its side purlins. Another example is the southern chancel roof at Ingatestone, the straight bracing of which, above its purlins, is visually in the nature of an afterthought.

V

During the Jacobean Period

Dovercourt church has a rood beam that was fitted during the reign of James I (1603–25), which is shown in Plate XVII. The double helices forming the relief decoration on the faces of the braces also determine the line of the edges, with the addition of a central pendant. The western face of the beam is carved with a trail of naturalistic grape vines having leaves but no fruit, reminiscent of the secular bressummers which were common from c. 1500 onward. The treatment of the quarter-round fillet at the upper corner of the beam is a repetitive and foliate relief, shallowly carved. The whole chancel roof at Ramsey is covered by plaster which leaves only its collars and braces with their principal rafters and the inner wall plates visible. The collars are braced, where they join the principals, by knees that are almost identical to the braces at Dovercourt (the preceding example), one of which is shown in Plate XVIII. The central pendant is repeated, and in the central area a lion-like face is carved. The lower edges of the collars are again quarter-rounded, and the curved surface is carved with an egg-and-tongue type of ornament that is too widely spaced to conform to classical prototypes. The chancel windows are dated to 1597 (Sir N. Pevsner, 1954, 128).

The chancel roof at Chipping Ongar has been described already with reference to the Norman period and to two subsequent frames that it incorporates. It must now be discussed again because the final repair to its three ancient systems of roofing was dated to the middle of the 17th century. This repair was effected by building three principal-rafter couples under the earlier roofs in order that side purlins could be introduced—to support the older common couples. The central pair of principals is shown in Fig. 37. It is arched to the central pendant which is carved with initials, W S, and dated to either 1642 or 1643—the figures are not easily read. The wall plate that was fitted at this date is curiously sectioned, as is shown in the drawing; and it was inserted mainly to mask from view the inner ends of the ancient sole pieces. The final example in this series is that shown in Plate XIX, which is that over the nave at Feering. The side purlins of this roof are butted; that is, they stop against the rafters and are tenoned into them; and this is also true of the common rafters which are made in short lengths, all tenoned into the purlins. The decoration of the straight tie beams, with deeply-carved lozenges and a wheat-ear pattern on their undersides, is without precedent among the examples described and does not derive from the previous decorative treatments. The date of this roof is uncertain, but it may well be late in the century.

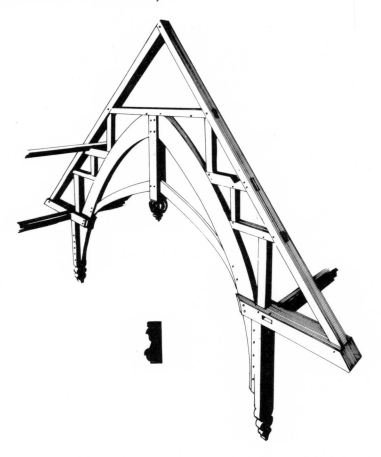

Fig. 37. The 1643 reinforcements of the chancel roof at Chipping Ongar

Roof framing during the 17th century was invariably of the side-purlin type, sometimes with numerous purlins in each slope of the roof; these purlins were butted or carried through as available timbers dictated or suggested. The dated specimen at Ongar, for example, has through purlins, since these must have been easier to insert beneath the ancient frame than butted ones would have been, but apart from this structural consideration the arched couples there have a curious appearance. The secondary curved braces, that converge on the long pendants, can have no functional significance, and the moulded wall plates serve mainly to cover what was thought unsightly; it therefore seems that values were uncertain in the mid-17th century. Good craftsmen in timber must have been abundant during this period, but works such as that at Ongar indicate that construction had ceased to be identified with ornament, and that the latter was no longer an aspect of construction.

VI

Summary

No actual date can be suggested at which timber framing could have been professionally assembled by a skilled minority of craftsmen, but a Danish author (E. Møller, p. 17) states that the possibilities existed for a highly developed timber-framing tradition at the beginning of our historical dating period. It is less perplexing in the light of this statement to find that the two oldest examples of timber work found among the Essex churches are so dissimilar and originate in seemingly unrelated traditions. These two are both Anglo-Saxon and are the churches of Greensted and Hadstock. The Greensted building, with its walls of vertical split logs with fillets set into their grooved edges, is an example of a type well known in Denmark during the 9th century and for a long time previously. Carpenters' joints were used to a considerable extent there, yet were combined with the archaism of split half-logs set upright to form walls requiring no cladding—but possibly, as Ray suggested, these were concealed by plaster or lime cement. Unfortunately we cannot tell what sort of roof it had, beyond the recorded fact that it was thatched, and its doors are also an unknown quantity.

The door and window frames at Hadstock are sophisticated in contrast to Greensted's walls, and the technical knowledge involved would derive from Roman precedents that had spread with Christianity. The construction of the door relates closely to the construction of clincher-built ships, as do its fastenings of iron, which are the same as the copper clenches still used at the present time by boat builders who work in the traditional methods of that craft. The ribs used in such small craft are commonly half-round in section, and are similar to the ledges of the Hadstock door which are nearly circular in section. It is possible that the monarchs of the later Saxon times could command both good craftsmen in timber (Hadstock is evidence to this effect) and designs of literally Romanesque style.

After the Norman Conquest examples of carpenters' work are a little more numerous, so far as surviving pieces are concerned, and the apsidal roof at East Ham, dated to *c.* 1130, is probably a good representative in view of its proximity to London. It is largely mortise-and-tenon jointed and also makes use of the bridle joint to some extent, but it is just as difficult to relate to other buildings as are the preceding examples, because too few buildings of such age survive in Essex. The Norman church at Chipping Ongar retains seven couples of its chancel roof that may well date from its foundation or consecration, which are of a type that could be braced after they had been reared, as a couple. The ashlar pieces and the collar braces are butt-notched, and pegged through their faces when in position, as is illustrated in Fig. 1. The method is recorded in France between *c.* 1190 and *c.* 1250 by Henri Deneux, and an example at Mittelzell has been proved to date from 1234, but there is no reason why the Ongar roof should not be older than the others since, as Dr. Saeftel states (1970, 164): 'England may be regarded as a special development centre for all areas in N W Europe'. This was said in relation to cruck roofs but I see no reason why it should not apply to other techniques, and one more will be suggested later.

The Ongar roof was not a good one in any sense, and it is probably due to the weakness of this type that so few examples have survived. The outward spread of the rafters' feet had, in these cases, to be withstood entirely by the masonry walls, and all components beneath the collars were considered to be in compression as a result. Many walls must have collapsed as a result of this roofing design during, or quite soon after, the Norman period. No single and predominant type of framing seems to appear in Essex until buildings and roof frames with notched lap jointing became numerous. The Rhenish helm spire of the late Saxon tower at Sompting, Sussex, has squinting lap joints without notching (C. A. Hewett, 1980, 289, fig. 311), and some re-used timbers at West Bergholt seem to witness the introduction of relatively inefficient notching in c.1000 A.D. in this country. Examples of notched lap-jointed carpentry are quite numerous, and within the scope of the present work seven have been mentioned: Roydon nave roof, Navestock bell tower, Bradwell bell turret, Stanway roof couple, Ongar two roof couples, Upminster spire and Wethersfield spire, and other examples are known that are not in churches. This distinctive and easily recognisable type of carpentry is most frequently found in association with the Early English period; its origins are not as yet known, but the bulk of surviving evidence suggests a definite connection with the Saxon home-lands—together with a course of development in England.

It seems that scissor bracing was introduced into Essex roofing at about the same time that secondary rafters were being used in hall and barn roofs, that is, during the early 13th century, and that this type of roof may also be identified with the Early English period. It was also during this period that the notch, or V-shaped, features of the lap joints were disguised, hidden from view by a thin covering flange of timber, and these are termed 'secret' notched laps. This may, again, be an English contribution to carpentry, since no European examples of the technique have been published. The earliest examples of this jointing are those in the roof of the capella-extra-muros at Little Coggeshall which are dated from c. 1220. It was towards the close of this period that lap jointing was superseded by tenoning, and that the introduction of both curved and crooked timber took place. At Wethersfield only four curves appear above the floor of the bell chamber, strongly contrasting with the straight timbers used for all other purposes, while towards the close of the 13th century, in Stifford spire, the curved timbers had become the majority of those used.

This was a striking change of material, and it is the most noticeable event in the early history of carpentry in Essex. The use of bent timber did not directly affect the designs of roof frames, since it was used to modify the appearance of well-tried designs, such as that with seven cants, of which early bent-wood examples are the roof over the north aisle at Danbury and others at Beeleigh Abbey and Rettendon church. The principle of doubly framing roofs, that is, framing both across the building and also along it, seems to have been introduced in the second half of the 13th century, in the manner seen at White Roding. From that time, c. 1260-80 onwards, roof framing in Essex had, so far as the examples show, an equal number of adherents for its two forms—single or double framing. The bell turret at Aythorpe Roding represents the Early English period, and can be seen to derive directly from the Norman turret at Bradwell, the structural design of the one being translated into curved timbers for the later Roding example.

44

I. Roydon, St. Peter's Church.

II. Fingringhoe, St. Ouen's Church.

III. Fingringhoe, St. Ouen's Church.

IV.   Ridgewell, Church of St. Laurence.

V.   Stebbing, St. Mary the Virgin, Chancel.

VI. Kelvedon, St. Mary the Virgin.

VII. Steeple Bumpstead, Church of St. Mary.

VIII. Berechurch, St. Michael and All Angels.

IX.   Gestingthorpe, Church of St. Mary.

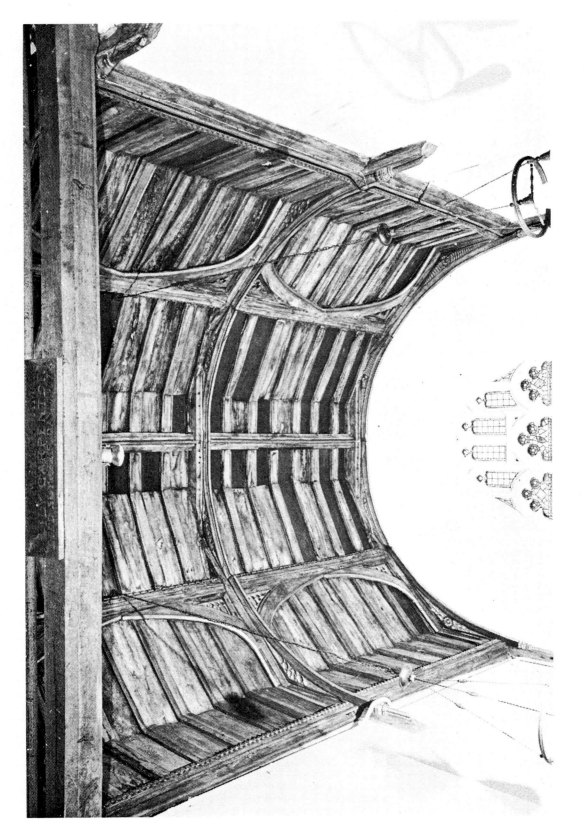

X. Laindon, St. Nicholas's Church.

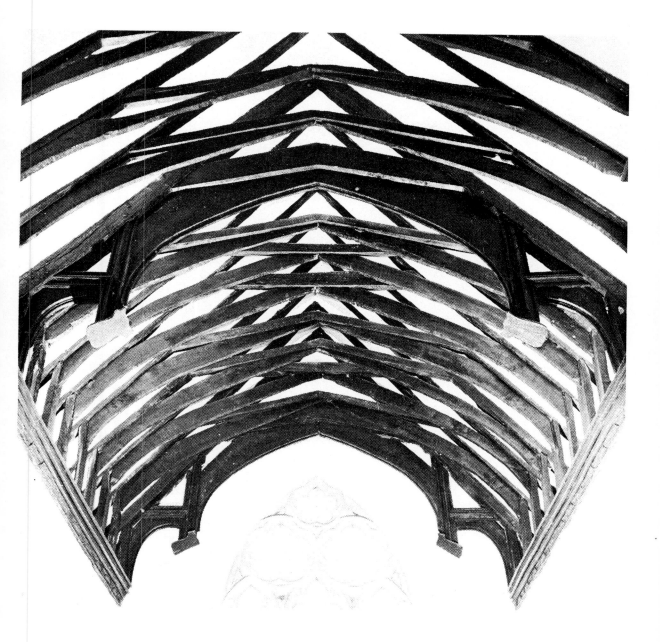

XI.   Little Hallingbury, St. Mary the Virgin.

XII. Saffron Walden, Church of St. Mary the Virgin.

XIII.   Saffron Walden, Church of St. Mary the Virgin.

XIV.   Bocking, Church of St. Mary.

XV. Castle Hedingham, St. Nicholas's Church.

XVI. High Easter, St. Mary the Virgin.

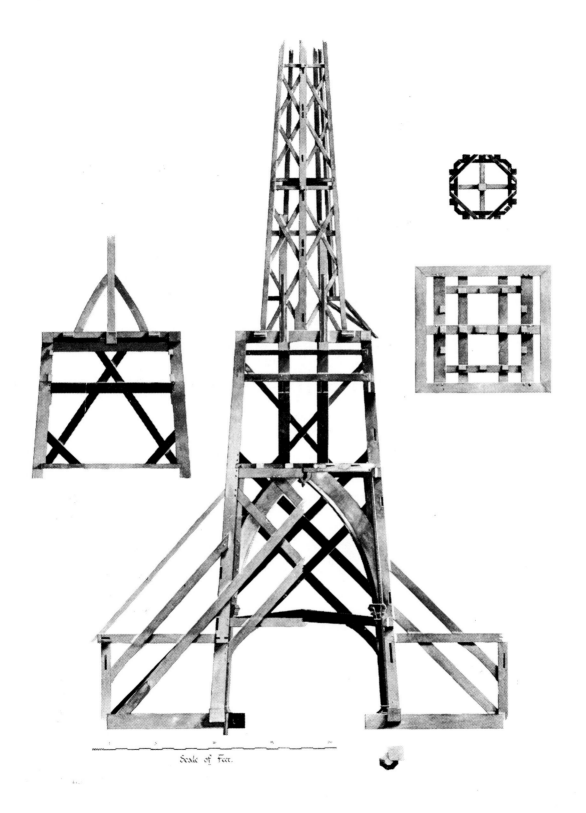

Scale of Feet.

XXI. Navestock, St. Thomas the Apostle.

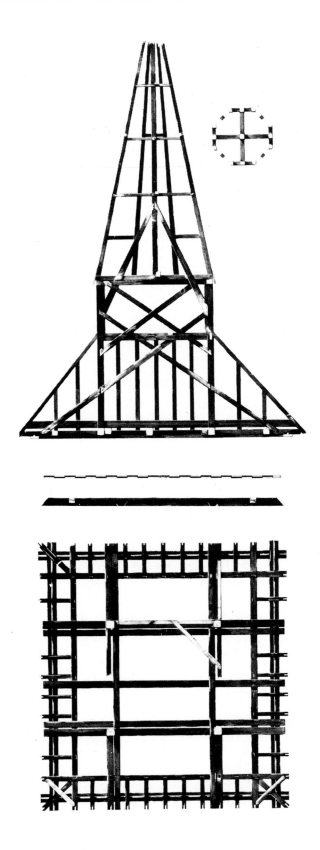

XXII. Upminster, Church of St. Laurence.

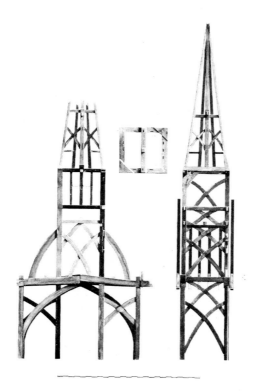

XXIII.   Little Burstead, Church of St. Mary.

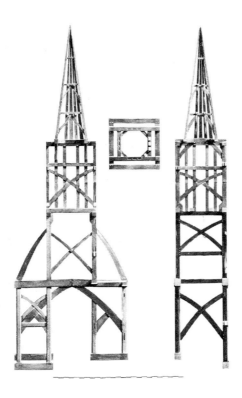

XXIV.   Black Notley, Church of St. Peter and St. Paul.

XXV.   Laindon, Church of St. Nicholas.

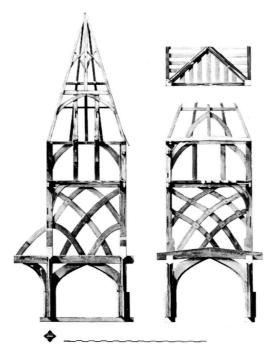

XXVI.   Horndon-on-the-Hill, Church of St. Peter and St. Paul.

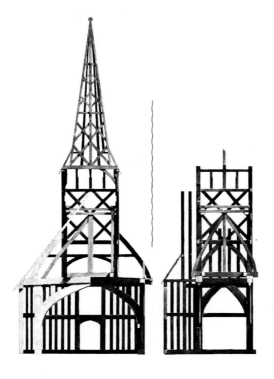

XXVII.   Ramsden Bellhouse, St. Mary's Church.

XXVIII. Bulphan, St. Mary's Church.

XXIX.　Bocking, Church of St. Mary

XXX.   Finchingfield, Church of St. John.

XXXI. Waltham Abbey.

XXXII.   Liston, Chancel.

XXXIII.　Little Bentley, Nave.

XXXIV. Sheering, Nave.

During the following Decorated period, the use of curved timber was fully expounded in Essex when examples, such as the nave roof at Foxearth supported on a massive timber arch, were framed; this, being a roof type that was highly efficient, continued to be used at least until the dated frame at Ongar of 1643. No clear reason for the combination of the two traditions—those of straight, and of bent timber—can be defined; but the existence of such roofs as that at Cressing, which ultimately resulted from this combination, supports the view that it resulted from the intention to produce new types by the mixing of old ones. During this period collar-arched and crown-post roofs were built in nearly equal numbers, some doors were constructed in the light of extremely clear thinking like that at High Roding, and porches were built in their earliest forms. The oldest *type* of porch is that at White Notley which has scissor-braced rafters, and a succeeding type is that represented by the porches at Frating and Aldham, which makes a conspicuous feature of S-curved timbers, used to support the collars as ogee arches. These are considered by Saeftel (Dr. F. Saeftel, 1970, 167) to stem from cruck building, and to represent a style of bent-wood construction that originated in England and later spread to northern France. He dates its beginnings as during the 11th century. Belfries of this time were various in form, comprising four-post towers like that at Stock, portal-framed with turrets like that at Notley, and complicated towers like that at Laindon, which incorporates 'syles', or A-frames.

Crown-post roofs and roofs with seven cants in single framing both continued to be built until about the middle of the 15th century, and the arched-to-collar roof was combined with both central and side-purlin types as well as being modified, as at Birdbrook, into an eaves-bladed form—which according to Saeftel relates to the 'knae-hus' originating in Jutland and terminating in the 'legender-stuhl' of Germany. During the second half of the 15th century panelled roofs also appear, framed in six cants like that at Stebbing; in these the collar purlin was retained as a butt purlin fitted between the bay collars, as at Great Horkesley. A delight in display arose during the final quarter of the 15th century, which is evident in those doors which are traceried but poorly framed, as at Shalford. Single and double hammer-beam roofs of magnificent appearance were built as the century drew to a close, as at Gestingthorpe and Hedingham, but their weaknesses are emphasized by the iron reinforcing ties that have been necessary in both churches. These roofs lack the strength of any great arch, like that at Westminster Hall or Gosfield church, and rely for their permanence on a succession of chase tenons at each side, which approximate to a weakened secondary rafter, or a deformed collar arch. Display was thus indulged at the expense of sound construction during the later Perpendicular years.

The finest contributions of the period to carpentry in Essex were the roofs that have been named camber-beamed. Excellent examples exist at Saffron Walden above both nave and chancel clerestories, which have suffered only from boring insects, being too direct and simple in design to fail mechanically. Aisle roofing of this type also exists, often magnificently carved, like that at Sible Hedingham and at Bocking. Other closely related specimens are those with very short queen posts, added to increase the pitches slightly, of which the richest example is over the nave clerestory at High Easter. Appropriately, the Perpendicular period seems responsible for the tallest and most impressive timber towers in Essex—the three examples being at Bulphan, Margaretting and Blackmore (Pevsner, 1954, 93, 268 and 76 respectively). The last named is the tallest and most elaborate, and has been described as 'one of the most impressive, if not *the* most impressive, of all timber towers of England' by Sir Nikolaus Pevsner, who has seen all the others and is in a position to judge the matter. Porch building also attained its most impressive form with the hammerbeamed example at South Benfleet, but it must be emphasized that not all works of the period were good, and many were both florid and decadent.

Some visually rewarding timber work was executed during the Jacobean period, notably the chancel roof at Ramsey church, which features double helices as the main decorative treatment; and some Renaissance motifs, like the egg-and-dart, began to appear in timber carving. The porch at Mundon, while its date is uncertain, provides a rich example of timber building and one which incorporates almost every feature, structural and decorative, that was to prevail throughout the 17th century in domestic front elevations. The nave roof at Feering is possibly the latest piece of expensive and highly decorated carpentry surviving in Essex churches and, since it has mainly geometrical ornament, it may date from the second half of the 17th century. Two nave roofs of the 18th century survive, at Berden and Bradwell-juxta-Mare; both have king posts and raking struts and their collars were mortised to hold ceiling joists.

Chapter Three

Timber Porches

From the Decorated to the Jacobean Period

The timber porches of some Essex churches are complete buildings like one-roomed houses, with walls, fenestration, vergeboards and roof frames all conforming to the general trends that have been described already, with regard to roofing. The oldest ones are of the 14th century and it may be that they constitute the beginning of the tradition, rather than its oldest survivors. A porch was ordered to be built for Westminster Hall, by Henry III in 1244, and Salzman (L. F. Salzman, 1952, 95) states that a large part of the marriage service took place there, while the church porch was often specified as the place where debts or other payments were to be made. Later, and with regard to the year 1447–8 from the records of Eton College, Salzman (1952, 523) quotes that '. . . in the south side of the bodie of the chirch a faire large dore with a porche ouer the same for christenyng of childre and weddynges' existed or was built. It seems, therefore, that few porches existed other than those commanded by kings during the 13th century, and the early 14th-century specimens described probably represent the beginnings of this part of church carpentry.

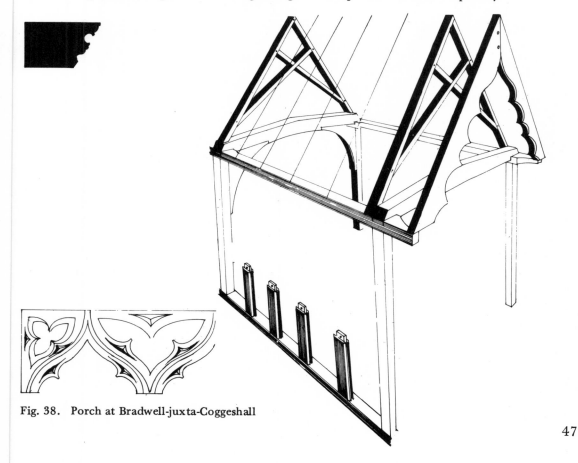

Fig. 38. Porch at Bradwell-juxta-Coggeshall

Fig. 39. Porch at Frating

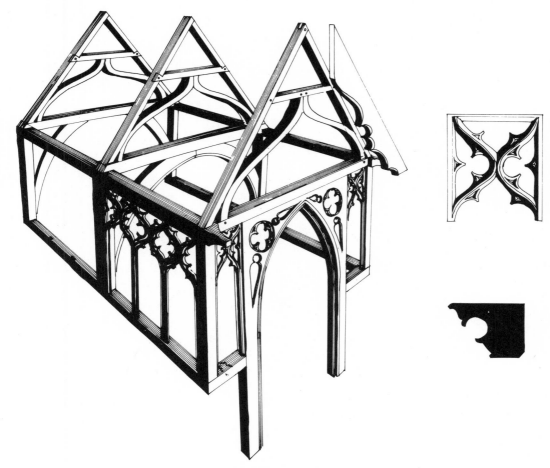

Fig. 40.   Porch at Aldham

The south porch of the church at Bradwell-juxta-Coggeshall is a mixture of items from widely differing points in time, and these include turned balusters of late 16th-century character which support some planks of 14th-century tracery—a mixture of considerable visual charm. Its roof, however, is of importance for this present purpose since it comprises six couples that are scissor-braced—without collars—by means of chase tenons. These rafter couples could represent the final quarter of the 13th century, and whilst they more probably form a late rural usage of this construction type, they do also provide a single specimen that can be stated with conviction to predate, typologically, all the others. (See Fig. 38.) This fact enables us to trace developments from a known point. The next two examples, illustrated in Figs. 39 and 40, are from Frating and Aldham, respectively. Both are of the 14th century, and the tracery of the latter dates from the Decorated period. Its roof couples, like those of Frating, show a strange form of the arch-braced collar type, emphasizing the re-curved or sinuous line of the ogee. The deeply hollowed moulding that is shown in black on Fig. 40 is the one which runs right round the arched timbers—or durns—which form the south doorway at Aldham. A date of c. 1330 is proposed for this example.

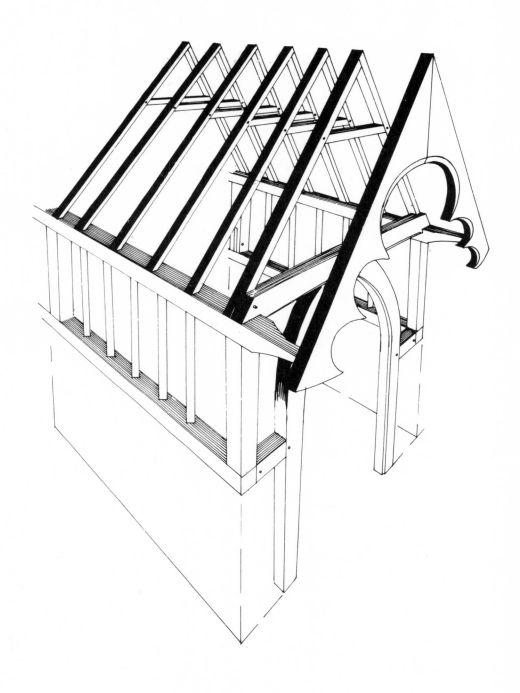

Fig. 41.   Porch at White Notley

50

A similarly early porch is that to the south entrance of the church at White Notley, illustrated in Fig. 41. It would probably date from the second half of the 14th century, and its roof couples with their collars have an archaic appearance. The extremely boldly cusped vergeboards also look archaic, but such cusping does

Fig. 42. Part of the porch at Radwinter

appear early in manuscript illuminations and this porch, therefore, may be older than suggested. But for the drastic 'restoration' during the 19th century, Radwinter's south porch would have been a serious contender for the title of 'most impressive timber porch in Essex', but only the base has survived with a dragon-beamed and jettied first floor. This is illustrated in Fig. 42, since nothing similar has survived elsewhere in the county.

Fig. 43. Porch at Bradwell-juxta-Mare

The example at Bradwell-juxta-Mare which is shown in Fig. 43 relates structurally to the marriage-service purpose of the building, since it is open and traceried only at its entrance bay and weatherproofed at the bay nearest the south door of the church—these facts are shown in the drawing. The third quarter of the 14th century is a reasonable date for this example and the use of massive ogival arch heads does not conflict with such dating. The cross sections of a central post, and of a mullion, are given with one example of the side-light tracery. This porch was moved from the former church of St. Mary, at Shopland in Essex, which was demolished in 1957–8.

The porch shown in Fig. 44 is that to the south of Panfield church and it is believed to date from the central decades of the 15th century, as does the greater part of the church fabric. It is a most satisfying example with side-light tracery of excellent character, and a selection of mouldings, shown inset, are early examples of their types.

52

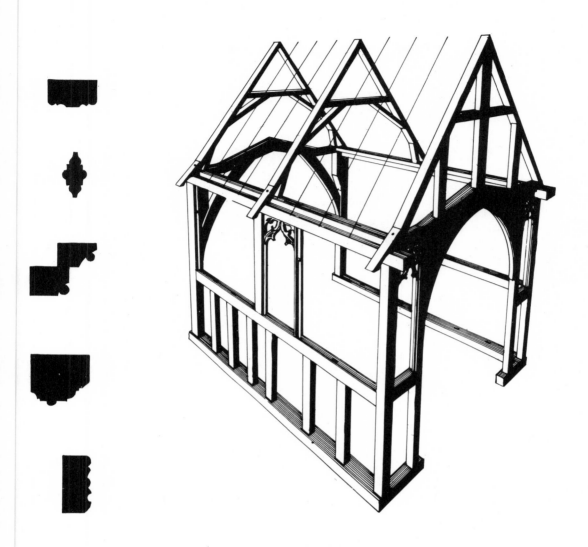

Fig. 44.   Porch at Panfield

Absolute pride of place must be given to the Benfleet porch which is illustrated in Figs. 45 and 46. This can have few, if any, serious rivals in the kingdom and constitutes a *tour-de-force*. Structurally it is too ambitious; the application of hammerbeams to so narrow a span of roofing cannot be justified and the result is slightly overweight when viewed from within. The blind tracery of the front-gable panelling is most successful, as is the unusual gambrel-roof shape given by the verge-boards. These are shown projected to the right of the drawing. The remarkably deep and finely cut traceries of the eight lights provided each side are the nicest portions, visually, of this example. A section of a hammerbeam, a mullion, and a central post are given in silhouette in Fig. 46. The date for this work is most probably quite late in the 15th century, during the final quarter.

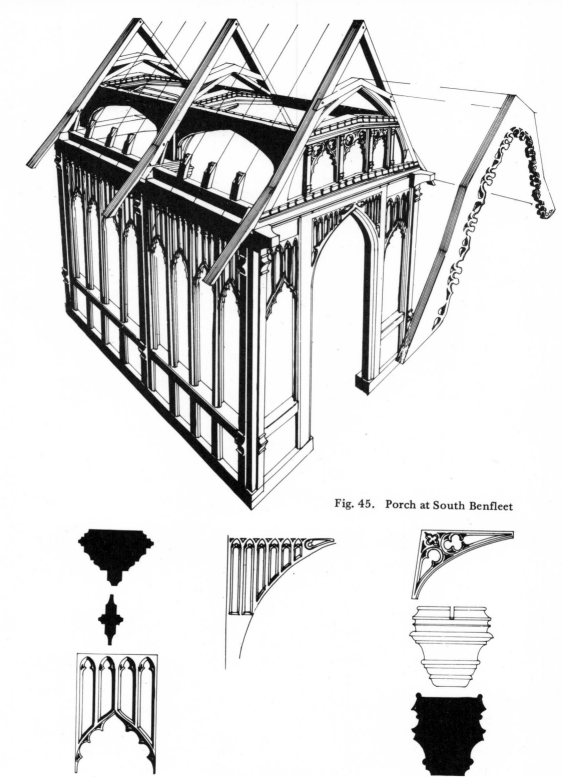

Fig. 45.   Porch at South Benfleet

Fig. 46.   Details from the Benfleet porch

54

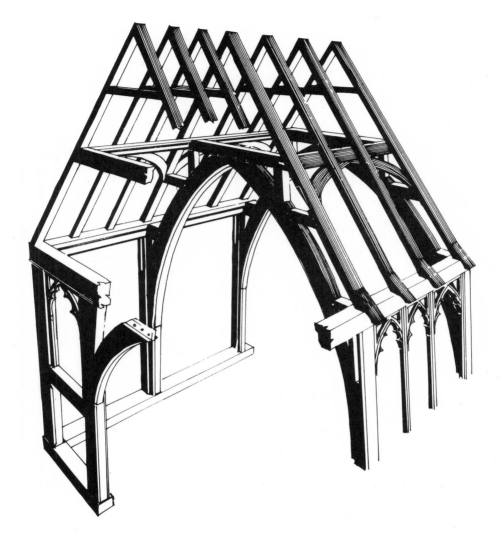

Fig. 47. Porch at West Hanningfield

The West Hanningfield porch is shown in Fig. 47. It is structurally of the same type as the example at Horndon-on-the-Hill, being arched to the collars and spur-tied. This is a roof type reminiscent of that over the nave at Cressing and a similar dating would be logical—the second half of the 15th century, and probably the final quarter. A finer point at West Hanningfield is the fact, which is evident, that the carpenter who built the porch believed absolutely in the type of roof frame he employed, since he did not use a tie beam for the inner frame abutting the southern wall of the church. It was not uncommon to build porches of brick, and some of these were given timber roofs, like the one at Takeley, shown in Fig. 48. This is a heavily framed crown-post assembly, and a roof that is stylistically backward looking; a date of *c.* 1500 is proposed for it.

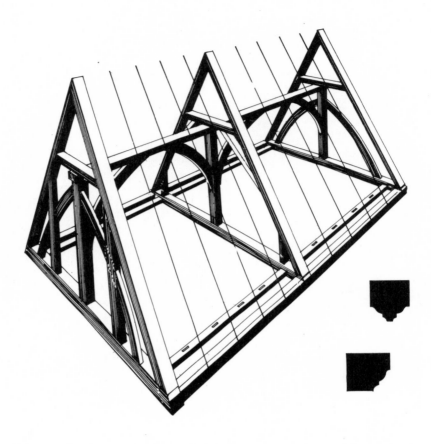

Fig. 48. Roof of porch at Takeley

The church at Runwell has two fine timber porches—one to the north which is illustrated in Fig. 49, and another which is very similar, to the south. The decorative details include both Tudor roses at the centres of the tracery quatrefoils (shown inset), and a niche on the crown stud for the display of a pre-Reformation statuette. The spandrel at the left side of the four-centred arch to the northern porch is inscribed with the name 'IOhe . . . Abbott' and what may well be a date placed between the two names, but this is too difficult to decipher. The north porch at Margaretting, as shown in Plate XX, is an example of similar date to the Runwell specimen.

56

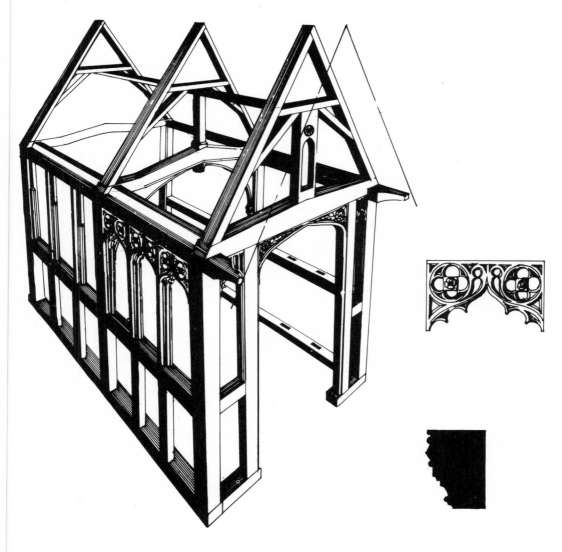

Fig. 49. Northern porch at Runwell

The porch at Bulphan (Fig. 50) is Tudor and late Perpendicular, combining these two styles into an appearance that, among the timber porches in this county, is very unusual and satisfying. Structurally the roof is king post and ridge piece, with common rafters tenoning into the ridge in the manner used frequently for the later examples of hammerbeam roofing, like those at Wrabness and Little Bentley. The tracery in the side lights is curiously fitted above four-centred arches, and the vergeboards—a piece of one of which is shown inset—are so dissimilar to other examples in Essex that a London carpenter of some repute may have been engaged for this work. One of the longest porches in the county is of similar date and plainer treatment—that at Doddinghurst, illustrated in Fig. 51, which shows half its length. A date of *c.* 1530 is suggested for this specimen, which had grooved studs for its tongued panels—the same method of walling that was employed at Margaretting.

Fig. 50.   Part of the porch framing at Bulphan

The porch shown in Fig. 52 is the one at Marks Tey. It is probably all of one build and dating from the middle decades of the 16th century, which ascription (if acceptable) renders the chamfered and diagonally-set mullions at each side unusually interesting, since they have a 17th-century appearance. The only truly 17th-century porch in Essex is that shown in Fig. 53—the north porch at the now derelict church of Mundon. The use of wind bracing in the lower walls to maintain the porch in contact with the masonry of the nave wall is both unique and satisfying, functionally. The flattened and four-centred knees beneath the front tie beams are still carved with the trailing vine leaf, implying that this must have been an early

58

Fig. 51. Part of porch at Doddinghurst

essay in the Jacobean style of treatment, and *c.* 1600 is suggested. The pendants are octagonal, and the gable finial, which is the original, is square. The various profiles of its members, which are shown in silhouette, are rather unusual combinations of normal Perpendicular forms such as the beaded casement, and numerous roll mouldings.

Porch building, as these few examples show, reflects the overall developments of timber framing; that is, in framing walls, the tying of roof frames and the progression of mouldings and tracery styles. The roof types used included examples of the main stream of development starting with chase-tenoned scissor bracing at Bradwell and progressing through arch-braced collars to crown posts, seven-canted roofs and,

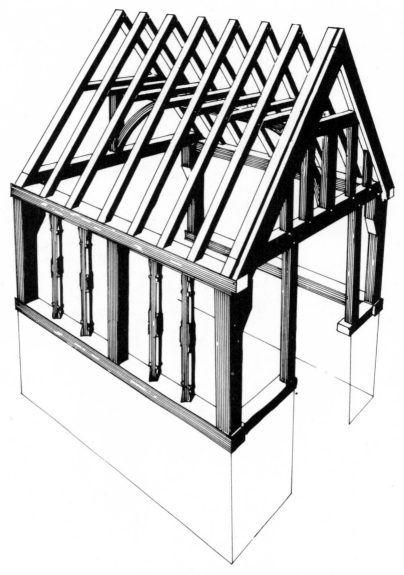

Fig. 52. Porch at Marks Tey

at the peak, hammerbeams at South Benfleet. The experimental period in roof framing, when the elements of the different types were combined into curiosities of great elaboration, like the nave roof at Cressing, also finds its way into porches with examples like that at West Hanningfield, arched to the collars with spur ties in addition to having side purlins and common collars—all of which verges on the excessive use of means. It seems that a majority of carpenters kept their porch roofs reduced to a minimum of members, like the common-collared roof over the two-bay porch at Doddinghurst, realising that these miniature buildings were not naves on a small scale, but structures that were inherently more stable, since they were built with timbers that were heavier than the dimensions of the buildings necessitated.

Fig. 53. Jacobean porch at Mundon

Ultimately the porch of apparently secular design appeared, as at Marks Tey, which lacks tracery or any other feature that could indicate that it was not a farmhouse porch, and the last example which is the uniquely elaborate porch at Mundon, wherein the pendant motif appears in porch building. As always, dates are uncertain so far as porches are concerned, and the Mundon specimen incorporates decorative details which could place it in the 16th century, but the totality of such features, together with the extreme flatness of the arches, seems to indicate c. 1600 with some probability. The use of re-curved timbers like those at Frating and Aldham can be related to the cruck-timber tradition of England, as indeed Dr. Saeftel has pointed out (Dr. F. Saeftel, 1970, 46) and the frequent use in early times of pairs of durns from a split trunk is also related to cruck methods of building.

61

Chapter Four

Spire and Belfry Framing

There is little room for doubt concerning the date of the timber tower at Navestock, which has been previously publicised, and also carbon dated by the University of California, in 1963. The carbon date obtained by Professor Fergusson was: age 770 ± 60 years, indicating an erection date of 1193. This was a free-standing timber tower when built, as is shown in Plate XXI. It is framed round four corner posts which are canted inward and elaborately braced with numerous long and slender timbers halved past both horizontal and vertical members, and secured in open notched-lap joints at their ends. The actual bell turret was designed to carry three bells swung on an east to west axis, and built with only one sound vent—a west-facing window from which both head timber and cill are now missing. The south aisle of the church was built later, during the Early English period, *c.* 1250, and at this time the eastern wall of the timber turret was used as a support for the rubble masonry of its western gable. All this is clear to view within the turret. It is the only surviving timber tower of the county that is so ancient as to be framed with notched lap joints. Some are known to exist, however, in other counties of England.

Pursuing this form of construction, the next example is the belfry at Bradwell-juxta-Coggeshall, which is shown in Fig. 54. This occupies the western bay of the nave of the Norman church, and is supported by a portal frame at the east. During the 14th century the eaves of the nave were raised, and at the same time the two posts of the portal frame had to be lengthened—the square butt joints of which lengthening are shown in the figure. At this time the ends of the original Norman transom beam were left protruding from the outside of the rubble walls—as is also shown in Fig. 54. All of these visible facts provide uncommonly firm evidence for ascribing this belfry to the original building of the church, and as a result it may safely be assumed that both small west-gable turrets like this, and free timber towers like the previous one, were not uncommon in the churches of our Norman period. The actual bell turret at Bradwell, as shown in the drawing, was plain and box-like with a saltire pattern of thin bracing in each wall—again secured in open notched lap joints at their ends. No clear evidence has survived as to the form of sound vents, nor the number of bells originally provided, but two seem probable. The spire is not contemporary and lacks merit.

I

Early English

The next two structures with this type of carpentry are both timber spires that surmount masonry towers, at Upminster and Wethersfield. Of the former, Upminster,

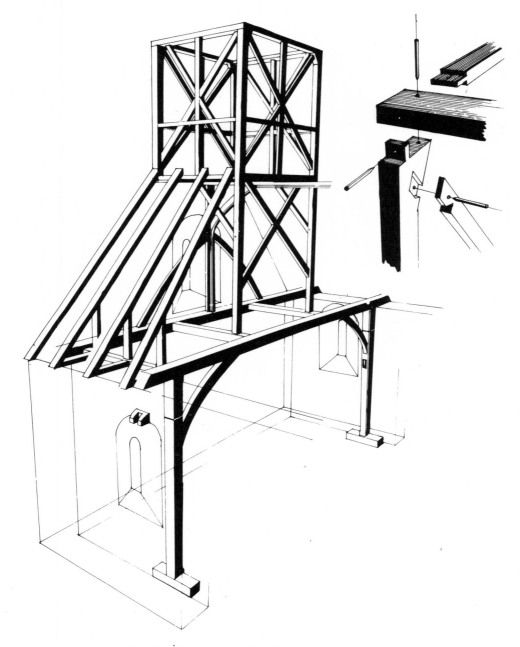

Fig. 54. Bell turret at Bradwell-juxta-Coggeshall

the Royal Commission stated that 'The West tower is of *c.* 1200; the bell-chamber is probably of rather later date'—and to the same date at this top stage of the masonry the timber spire must belong. The framing is shown in Plate XXII, which gives plan and elevation together with some details. All the timbers are entirely straight and of either square, or thin rectangular, section, the ends of the saltire

Fig. 55. Framing of the spire at Wethersfield

being retained in secretly notched lap joints, indicating, perhaps, a date of *c.* 1220 in view of their use in the Coggeshall Abbey roof already described. In this example the spire with its central 'mast' is original to the structure, and the whole provides an unusually complete example. The spire at Wethersfield, illustrated in Fig. 55, surmounts a masonry tower that the Royal Commission ascribed to the end of the 12th century. The drawing shows the upper part of this tower with its 12th-century pairs of lancet lights, and the platform of transoms and wall plates supporting the

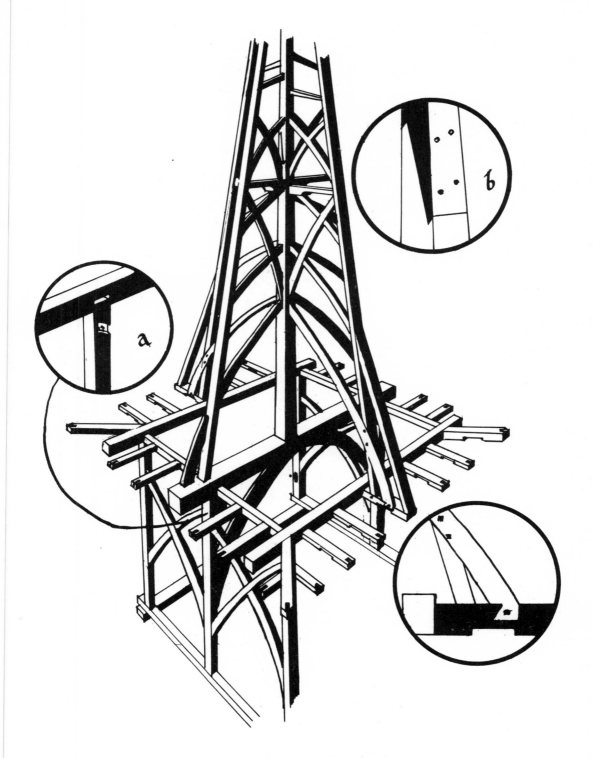

Fig. 56.   Framing of the spire at Stifford

pyramidal first stage of the spire, which is built in two parts like the preceding example. At Wethersfield all timbers are again entirely straight and square in section. Saltire bracing, which is interlaced in a most complex manner, is fitted all round the square part against which the pyramidal roof leans, and four secretly notched lap joints were used. A date during the second half of the 13th century is proposed for this spire. The 13th-century tower of the church at Stifford is surmounted by a timber spire of the same date, which is illustrated in Fig. 56. Several lap joints are used in the framing of this, but none are notched to resist withdrawal. Four of these joints are dovetails of the barefaced type, one of which is shown inset. The introduction of curvature in structural timbers is well illustrated by this example, which probably dates from the last quarter of the 13th century.

II

Decorated

The belfry at the west end of the nave at Aythorpe Roding is remarkable in that it is carried on a pair of transom timbers running from north to south, and there is no evidence for the normal posts to support these. Arch braces exist, as shown in Fig. 57, but it cannot be seen whether these fit into either posts or wall pieces

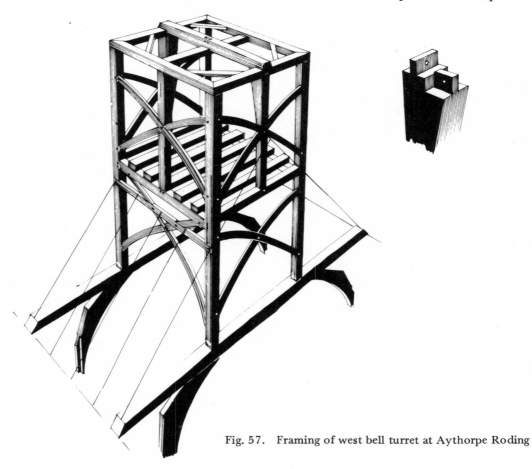

Fig. 57. Framing of west bell turret at Aythorpe Roding

66

owing to an excessive thickness of plaster, as at Dovercourt church. The entire fabric is ascribed to the 13th century, and it is logical to date the belfry from the initial building of the church. The central studs that are placed in each wall of the square turret obviously derive from the similar method used at Bradwell during the Norman period, and at Aythorpe they are crossed by curved saltire bracing. These studs have a form of jowl at their tops, which is designed to secure the ends of two crossed tie beams, on the intersection of which the spiremast stands. The tenons cut on these jowls are shown inset at Fig. 57. The extent to which curved timber is used for secondary purposes indicates a date of c. 1300 or the previous decade.

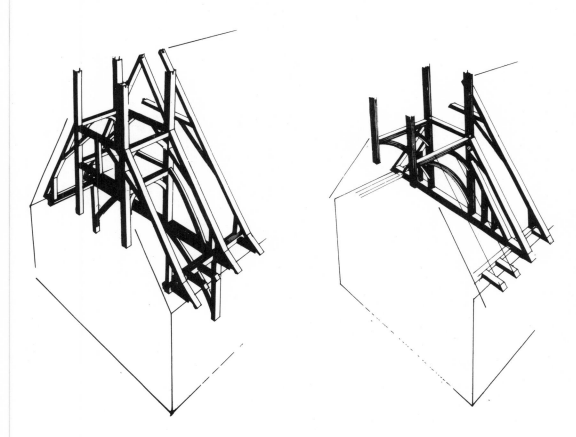

Fig. 58.   Frame of west bell turret at Magdalen Laver   Fig. 59.   Turret-framing at Little Leighs

The free-standing timber belfry at Little Burstead, illustrated in Plate XXIII, is an early example of the type that was based on a pair of portal frames standing astride the western bays of naves. It predates the nave roof there, and is later than the masonry carcase which is Norman and coarsed with indurated gravel, recently rendered over. The capstone of the original west gable still exists, and can be seen from inside the belfry; the position of this stone is marked by an 'x' drawn on the illustration. As is evident from this example, a vogue for complicated series of curved braces had begun. Two small examples, shown in Figs. 58 and 59, are from

Fig. 60.   Frame of belfry at Stanford Rivers

Magdalen Laver and Little Leighs respectively. It is probable that the example in Fig. 58 dates from the building of the roof of the nave, which is of seven cants with double collars; the 14th century is proposed for both roof and turret. The Little Leighs bell turret is very similar and mounted on a transom that has no wall pieces; the early 14th century is suggested for this example also.

Another free-standing portal-frame belfry of unusual construction is shown in Plate XXIV, which stands in the west end of the nave at Black Notley. Several peculiarities of framing exist, such as the rear frame wherein the two inner posts rise only to the arch braces; and the framing of the actual spire is effected without recourse to a central 'mast', which was the general practice from the earliest times. This is certainly a less rigid structure than any others examined, and the middle decades of the 14th century are a probable period for such experimental timber-work. The belfry at Laindon, shown in Plate XXV, is another highly complex structure, comprising two timber towers, one of which rises within the other and supports only the bells, while the outer one carries both turret and spire. There is one of the five transverse frames, the central one visible in the north–south section, which seems to echo the 'flowing' style of tracery, while the four posts carrying the bell frames are combined by straining beams into 'A' frames. The example at Stanford Rivers, shown in Fig. 60, conforms to the Decorated style of arcuation and includes the use of solid timber angles, or knees. This last feature, which was previously monopolised by shipwrights, was later to become common in land carpentry.

III

Perpendicular

The example shown in Fig. 61 is the belfry at Little Clacton, the upper parts of the turret of which have been replaced; the roof of the nave does not relate to the belfry, structurally, and the latter is a later intrusion into the church. One of the most remarkable of the timber towers is that illustrated in Plate XXVI. This is a remnant of a timber tower that evidently had an octagonal, or cruciform, ground plan when built; it has been cut down to fit between the nave arcades at some unknown date. Similar types, based on four posts, are numerous, and the octagonal plan seems to have been the normal one, as at Mundon and Navestock.

The arching of the numerous braces in the lowest stage of the Horndon example is four-centred, as may be seen in Plate XXVI, but functional considerations induced the carpenter to adopt a basic brace angle of 45° in most other situations, since flattened, or depressed, bracing is less stabilising in timber frames. The example shown in Plate XXVII is the belfry at Ramsden Bellhouse, based on two portal frames and incorporating arched braces of both Perpendicular and Decorated curvatures; the first helps to date the structure and the second shows purely functional thinking. The important development in belfry building during the Perpendicular period was the introduction of the type illustrated in Plate XXVIII, which is the example at Bulphan, whose original spire is now missing. Three towers of this type survive, at Blackmore, Margaretting and the present example—Bulphan. They extend the naves of the churches westward and are designed as very closely-set portal frames, elaborately stabilised by shores, arch braces and saltire bracing.

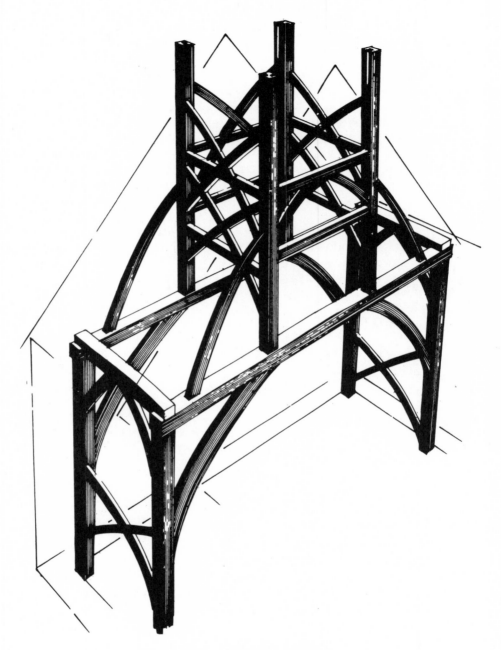

Fig. 61.   Frame of belfry at Little Clacton

The turrets of these three examples have features in common, most important of which is the use of one continuous sound vent that was traceried with pierced plank right round the four sides of the turrets. The type of housings for the continuous cill to this void can be seen in the illustration.

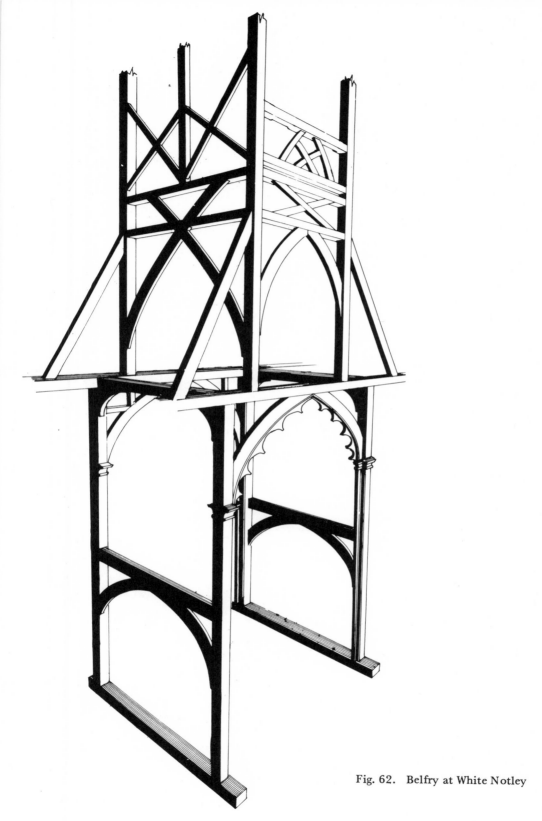

Fig. 62.   Belfry at White Notley

71

The example shown in Fig. 62 was built during the reign of Henry VII into the western bay of the 13th-century nave arcades of White Notley; for this reason its first-stage posts are unusually tall. The arch bracing employed in the lower, visible stage is all of four-centred curvature, with cusping applied to the eastern arch and capitals applied to the four posts. The construction of the second stage, which is the turret, is curious, as may be seen in the illustration, and it is not an entirely logical one (the eastern bell frame is shown), since it is integral with the turret wall in this case. The structure shown in Fig. 63 is literally a timber tower, standing on a base storey of flint flush work dated 1527 above its four-centred western doorway; this example is at Little Totham. The bracing forms arches of the purely functional character based on the angle of 45° but for the pair of braces forming an arch toward the nave of Perpendicular type. The extra square frame projecting to the north of the cills accommodate the spiral stair. The framing of this example is not traditional since it does not resemble any of the bell turrets of the previously cited examples. The 17th-century timber tower shown in Fig. 64 is that built on top of the brick tower damaged during the Siege of Colchester in 1648 (Pevsner, 1954, 269). This is honestly and sparsely timbered, and clad entirely with vertical boards in the tradition of the home counties, and at the arris rail forming the coping timber these boards were stopped 'long and short' producing battlements. The louvred windows of the turret, two to each wall, have very flattened four-centred arch timbers. The spire is traditionally framed, round a vertical mast timber mounted on the elaborate frame shown in the drawing; all the numerous corner joints are effected by box tenons through mitred bridles.

The evidence of those belfries which have been described indicates that free-standing timber tower belfries like that at Navestock, and bell-turrets that protruded through roofs like that at Bradwell, were both being built with the complete assurance derived from previous experience during the opening years of the 13th, and the closing years of the 12th centuries. Both these examples were framed with an emphasis upon straight, saltire-wise bracing which was interlaced and retained at the ends in open notched lap joints. Joints of this category were used in England during the first half of the 13th century or earlier; and the type has been illustrated in Fig. 3 with regard to the chancel roof at Ongar. All other examples of notched lap jointing are of early dates and the origin of this technique has not yet been determined. A European influence may have been involved, via the known maritime trading between Anglo-Saxon England and the region of the Rhine estuaries (Postan, 1972, 209). Squinted lap joints without notching have been noted at Sompting, Sussex, and notched lap joints on re-used timbers at West Bergholt, Essex—the latter archae-ologically datable to c. A.D. 1000. The last-mentioned joints were experimental by their profile, which offered a minimal objection to withdrawal, and was also inherently weak and liable to rive if so stressed. By 1130, however, the Cistercians were using open notched lap joints with refined, and therefore stronger, angles of entry for their Abbey Barn at Coggeshall. Wells Cathedral was using these same refined lap joints for all of its high-roofs until the time when building ceased for the duration of the Interdict, 1209 until 1213, which last event provides a definite date for the introduction of the 'secret' notched lap, used for the roof of Coggeshall Abbey's chapel in c. 1220 (Hewett, 1980, 47, 83).

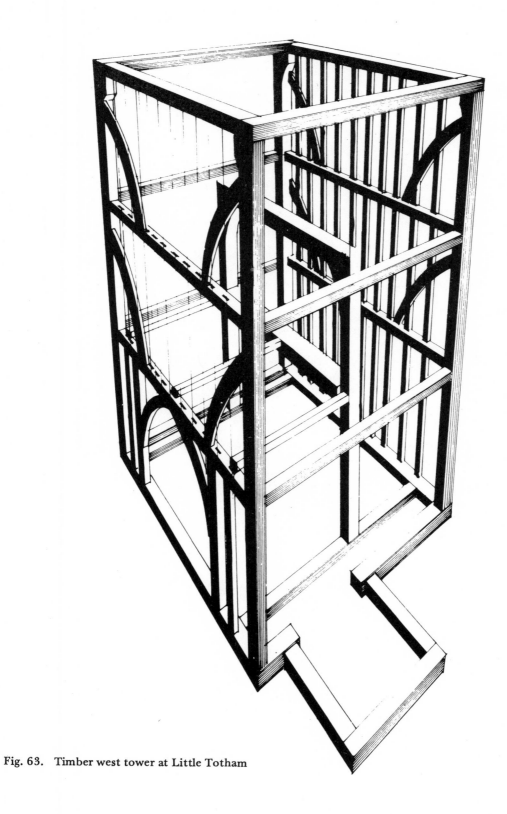

Fig. 63. Timber west tower at Little Totham

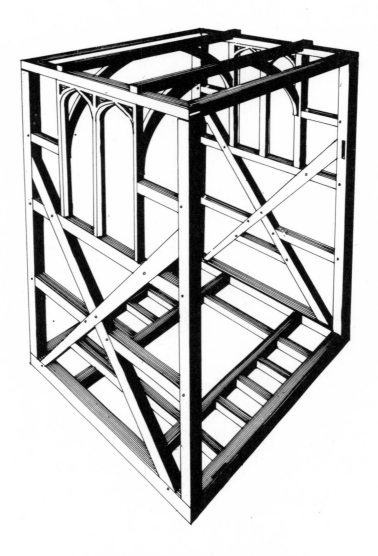

Fig. 64 a.   Timber tower at Marks Tey

The next two structures, the spires crowning the stone towers at Upminster and Wethersfield, are datable in that order by reference to their masonry and carpenters' joints. The earlier of these two is lavishly braced with saltire-wise straight timbers, of slender section, retained at their ends in the 'secret' form of notched lap joints in order that they might resist extension. This development of the joint has not yet been recorded in respect of any other European country, and is illustrated in Fig. 7, which shows the roof of the capella-extra-muros at Coggeshall Abbey, datable to c. 1220. The carbon-dated specimens of this joint are those in the Wheat Barn at Cressing, dated to *c.* 1255. At Upminster there are no curved timbers and a date somewhere near the middle of the 13th century is proposed. At Wethersfield only four secret notched laps were used, although the general design, with its reliance on complex series of saltire braces, in addition to its general similarity to the previous example, places it with some certainty in the final quarter of the 13th century. Some timber of naturally grown bent-shape arched braces was used in the lower seating of the spire. It is evident, therefore, that timber-framed spires were being built above three different kinds of substructure (timber towers, timber turrets and stone towers) during both the Norman and the Early English periods. It also appears that the introduction of curved timber occurred towards the close of the 13th century in Essex.

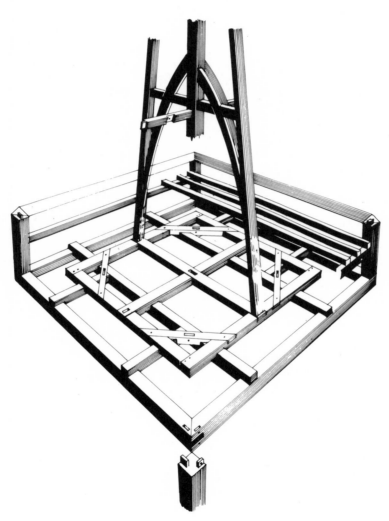

Fig. 64 b.   Framing of the spire at Marks Tey

The next example in this succession, which is the spire on the stone tower at Stifford, is probably of *c*. 1300, in view of the clearly contrasting extent to which curved timbers were used in its framing, and the survival therein of four lap dovetails at the feet of major braces, and lap-jointed ends to the curved pairs of saltire braces in its wall frames. An example of a turret, which dates to the ensuing quarter of the 14th century and which is of the type built earlier at Bradwell, protruding through the nave roof of its church, is the bell turret at Aythorpe Roding. This can be seen to derive directly from the Bradwell example, and possesses the same studs in the centre of each wall, crossed by saltire braces—the discontinuation of lap jointing and the use of curved timber being the main differences. Later, and probably during the Decorated period but towards its end, more elaborate belfries such as the Little Burstead one were being designed to transmit their weight directly down to the ground, rather than impose it upon the masonry shells of the churches.

The two examples which did transmit their weight to nave walls (those in Figs. 58 and 59) doubtless did so because both the churches and their turrets with bells were small, and not thought to overload the masonry. Both appear to date from the mid-14th century. The examples from this point forward: those from Notley and Laindon, Stanford Rivers and Clacton, show the continuation of the type that was borne on two portal frames, transmitting thereby its own weight to ground level. This type culminated in the examples at Leaden Roding and Cressing, both of which are relatively small and braced with timbers forming very depressed four-centred arches—neither of which is illustrated. The timber-tower type of belfry of which the earliest Essex survivor is that at Navestock, and which was framed essentially upon four posts which were either upright or inclined, also had a course of development which can be traced through the examples at Hanningfield, Stock and Mundon to the specimen shown in Plate XXVI which is at Horndon-on-the-Hill. This last, as its arch braces show in the lowest stage, is of the mature Perpendicular style, for which a reasonable ascription would be *c*.1500. The two forms, portal-framed bell turrets and four-posted, free-standing towers both had continual developments from the time, approximately, of the Conquest until the closing years of the Tudor period.

The innovation in this field of timber belfry building is that exemplified by the Bulphan specimen, which is one of three structures of its kind, all 15th-century, unusually impressive 'and massively timbered. The other two are at Margaretting and Blackmore, and each is designed as an extension to the length of the nave, which is continued as a form of timber arcade for a few short bays westward, having aisles to both north and south. They were apparently the ultimate development of medieval belfries in this county and all were fitted, originally, with one continuous sound vent which ran right round their turrets and had a continuous plank of tracery at the top of this, which was passed through the intervening vertical timbers. Two of these, at Blackmore and at Margaretting, have wooden tracery which has survived in its original situation; the first has four cinquefoiled lights and the second two trefoiled lights with mouchettes in their spandrels. All of them carried large numbers of bells.

Of the other belfries described, that at White Notley was designed, it appears, by a craftsman who probably specialised in these structures and yet tended to

76

perpetuate certain designs of long standing. It is not possible to decide from the structure at Little Totham, which is dated 1527, whether it is the work of a specialist carpenter or not. It closely resembles the framing of many tower-like timber dovecotes which exist in Essex, and does not seem to be a particularly specialised structure. The last example, that at Marks Tey dated from local records to 1648, is in contrast a purpose-built belfry structure recalling the saltire-braced framing of the oldest examples. The framing of its spire, shown separately, is very good but is not re-thought, being closely similar to some ancient examples. The four-centred sound vent heads look Elizabethan rather than mid-17 century.

Chapter Five

The Construction of Doors

The earliest door that has survived in Essex is that rarity still hung in the north doorway of St. Botolph's church, at Hadstock. This is Anglo-Saxon and probably of the first half of the 11th century. In Fig. 65, both outside and inside faces are shown, with a section of one of the long joints between its planks, and a perspective of the rivetting method used. The whole is of oak, with a steamed or dry-heated bend for the top 'ledge', and iron straps and rivets. The ledges, which are the bars affixed to the inside (the back of a door) are of three-quarter-circle section, and the iron rivets pass through them and are then spread against the lozenge-shaped iron washers which are wrapped round the ledges. This last detail is shown in the

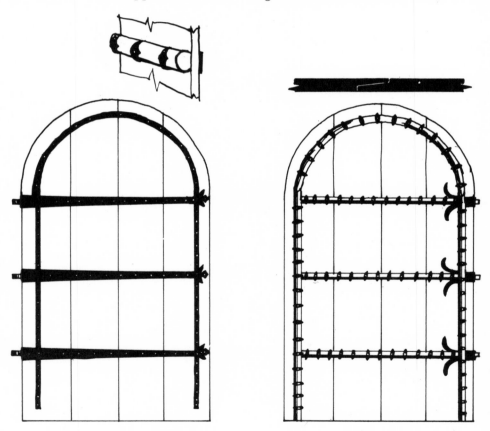

Fig. 65. North door at Hadstock

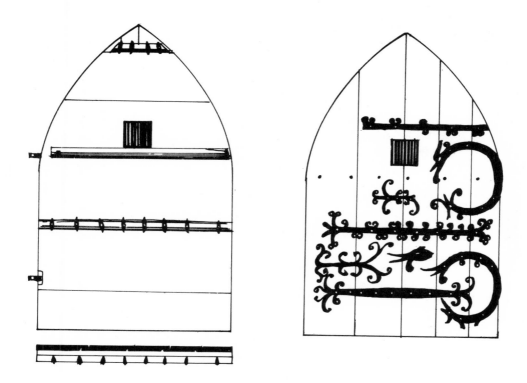

Fig. 66. North door at Buttsbury

perspective, inset. The long butted joints between the edges of the four planks are, sectionally, splayed rebates. One other door which is evidently of this great age is that shown in Fig. 66, the north door at Buttsbury in central Essex. It was originally made of five boards and had nearly circular ledges affixed to its inner surface by the same rivetting method as used at Hadstock. The planks in this second example also had splay-rebated joints like those at Hadstock, and the first construction, therefore, must also be ascribed to the beginning of the 11th century. Later, and probably during the Norman transitional period, this doorway was cross-planked—a process which half submerged its circular Saxon ledges—and the serpent-type ironwork was added.

The south doorway at White Roding church was ascribed by the Royal Commission to the 11th century. The tympanum of the doorway is carried by a wooden lintel, and the top of the door is square. It is made in four planks with square-edged butt joints and has ledges that are square with rounded arrises, which are affixed by wooden pegs with fox-wedged ends. All these details are shown in Fig. 67, with a fox-wedged peg inset. The joints between the planks are covered by iron strips that were nailed to each side of the abutments. The iron work has leaf ends, and is probably Early English for that reason.

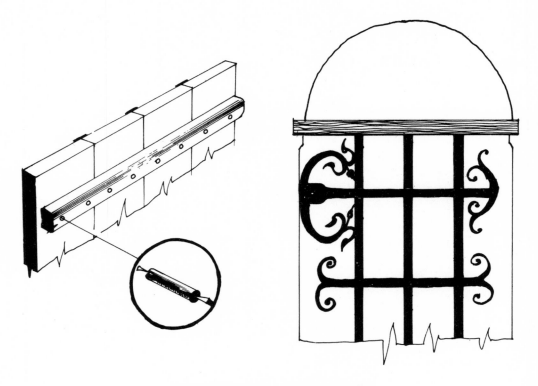

Fig. 67. Part of door at White Roding

Castle Hedingham church has no less than three doors dating from its Norman origin, and the probable date within that period is believed to be *c.* 1180. The best of these examples, all shown in Fig. 68, is that on the left of the drawing, the south door. The significant structural device here introduced is the use of counter-rebated plank edges, which in this case gives the long joints an embattled appearance.

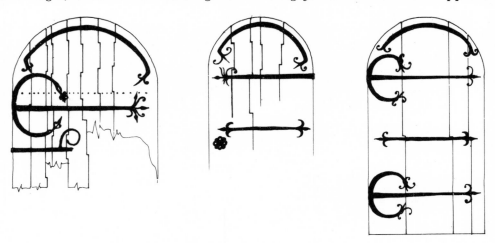

Fig. 68. Three doors from Castle Hedingham

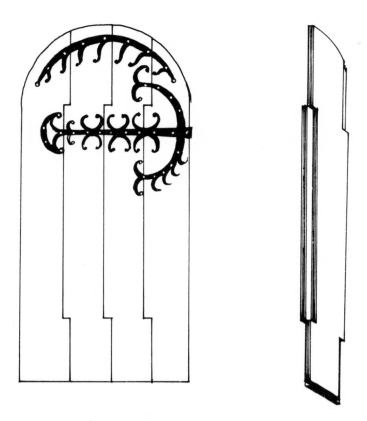

Fig. 69. North door at Elmstead Market

Another door of this type is the northern one at Elmstead Market, shown in Fig. 69, and in that drawing the exact nature of the counter rebates is shown at the right. It cannot be ascertained whether these doors had ledged inner sides, but it can be stated that with counter-rebated edges they would not need ledging, and their iron strapwork might have been adequate. The southern door at Heybridge is another ascribed to the 12th century by the Royal Commission, though it is very different, structurally, having square butt edges with square-sectioned ledges that are set into shallow housings that were cut across the width of the planks, and affixed by iron nails—the points of which were returned and re-driven. The last is the first example of the kind noted, as shown in Fig. 70.

The doors at Eastwood church, both north and south, are extremely fine with regard to their iron work. That in the north doorway is now un-hung, but fixed in place. It is therefore difficult to examine. The Royal Commission ascribed it to the late 12th century. The iron work affixed to its outer face, which is now inside the church, is rare in that it is fullered and swaged, as well as decorated with cold-set patterns. The south door of this pair is still on its hinges and all its structural detail can be examined; both its inner and outer faces are shown at the top of the drawing (Fig. 71), together with an edge section and a cross-cut section.

81

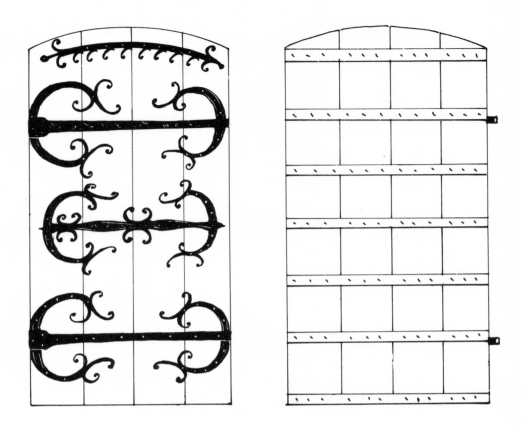

Fig. 70. South door at Heybridge

It is made in three oaken planks, the middle one being narrow with rebated edges, while the ledges (originally four in number) are of dovetailed cross section and tapered width. These were driven into dovetailed trenches cut across the backs of the planks. This is illustrated at the bottom and side of Fig. 71. The iron work is complex, seeming to relate to both 12th and 13th centuries: one of the straps bears a faintly decipherable inscription—'Pax regat intrantes eadem regat egredientes'—or 'May peace rule those entering and also those leaving', which is in Lombardic letters. The leaf shape beaten on the ends of the helical strapwork is that of the oak leaf. Both of these doors have been reduced in height, apparently because their lower parts had rotted.

The framing of the doors at Eastwood church has been found to have a cathedral carpentry precedent: the doors into the cloisters at Durham, the ledging of which is identical, and the rebated edges of the planks are similar—their date, however, is not known.

82

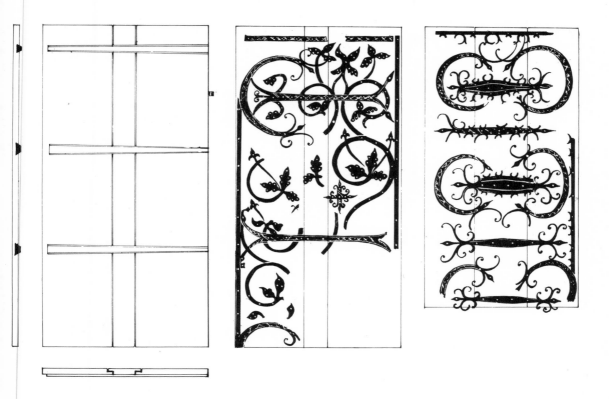

Fig. 71.   Eastwood: views of south and north doors

Two doors with entirely 'open' notched-lapped rear frames are now known to exist, at the cathedrals of Peterborough (west gates to the precinct), and the west doors at Selby Abbey, which last are dated to 'not later than 1170' by the published guide book to that abbey.

The next example illustrated, in Fig. 72, is the south door at High Roding; a church which the Royal Commission ascribed to the *early* 13th century, and its south 'door—framed and battened with ornamental iron work, 13th century' (R.C.H.M., 1921, 133). The strap hinges still retain the crescent, or anchor, pattern in a restrained form reconcilable with such a dating. The construction of this door is, again, unique. As is shown in the cross section beneath the outer face of the door at the right of the drawing, the vertical stiles and edge durns have V-grooved edges, while the ledges halved across them are of lesser thickness. These were set into their barefaced lap dovetails, only after which could the planks be slid into the V-grooves. The four planks, therefore, with their sallied or 'taced' edges, were slid into the frame last, towards the top of the door. The bottom rail or ledge was then fitted and pegged.

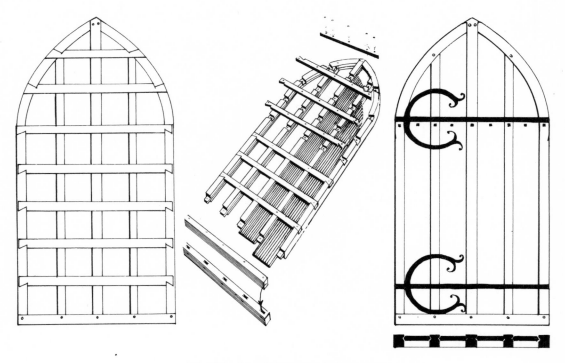

Fig. 72.   South door at High Roding

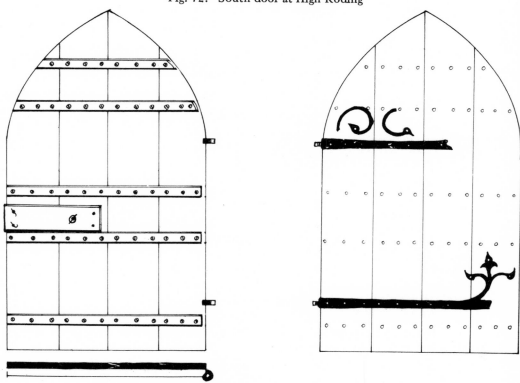

Fig. 73.   Outer face of south door at Ashen; centre section

84

Fig. 74. Outer face of door at Little Leighs
(Inset: stone moulding of door frame)

The south door at Ashen is of great interest, assembled with fox-wedged pegs that fix V-edged boards to square ledges with chamfered arrises. The few traces of iron strap hinges are shown on the drawing, Fig. 73. The Royal Commission ascribed this door to the 13th century, and this provides an example of V-edged boards that can be dated as early as *c.* 1300. A south door of very similar style is that at Little Leighs which is shown in Fig. 74. The woodwork of this door, including what survives of the rear frame, is unimpressive, but the two hinges with their foliated ends have an Early English style which is strong evidence for the blacksmithing being 13th-century. Strap ironwork, which is far more florid, has survived on the outer face of the original planks of the south door at Bocking, which is shown in Plate XXIX. There is no rear frame to this example, which has been 'restored'. The western door leading into the belfry at Navestock from the Early English south aisle there is hung in a stone doorway of the middle years of the 13th century. Since neither the stones nor the timbers have weathered, it is apparent that the pair of doors, together with their hinges, date from the same period as the aisle which was added in *c.* 1250. These doors are illustrated in Fig. 75.

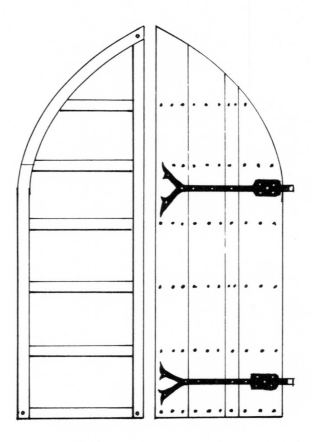

Fig. 75. Pair of doors from Navestock

An elaborate rear frame is that shown in Fig. 76, which is fitted to the south door at Belchamp Walter. The five boards are V-edged and pegged to the frame, the iron work is plain, but not in conflict with a mid-14th century ascription which is proposed. An ancient example of the unframed door, constructed of crossed boards spiked together, is that shown in Fig. 77. This is an old door re-used at the time of the rebuilding and placed in the base of the stone tower at Aldham church. The front boards have rebated edges, and those at the rear are square-edged. The Royal Commission ascribed this specimen to *c.* 1300. The remarkable door shown in Fig. 78 is the south door at Great Sampford, which was not dated by the Royal Commission, but its doorway was ascribed by them to *c.* 1300. There is no detail of either iron or timber work in this door to preclude its ascription to the same date. It is the most elaborate of all the saltire-braced doors in Essex, and it is pegged together; the boards have splayed and butted edges, as shown in the section, and its bottom rail is missing.

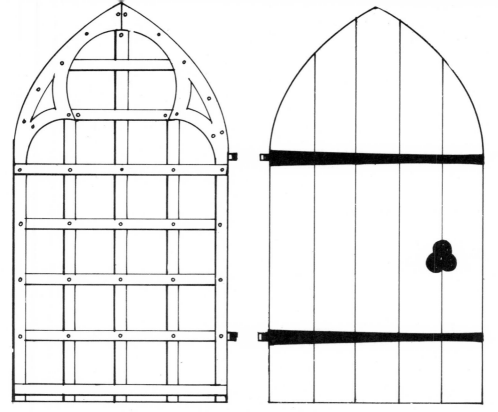

Fig. 76.   Inner face of south door at Belchamp Walter

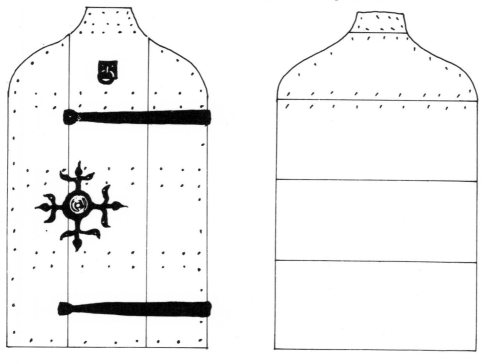

Fig. 77.   Aldham: door, re-hung in the tower

87

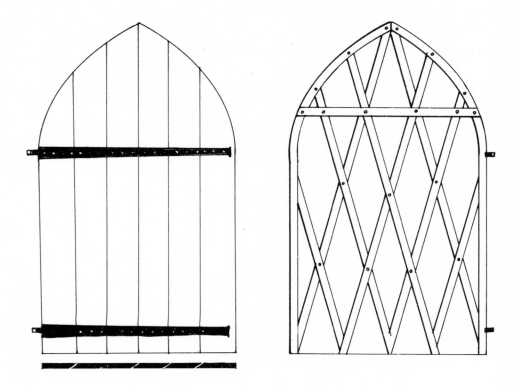

Fig. 78. South door at Great Sampford

The two timber doorways illustrated in Fig. 79 surround the masonry of the north and south doors at Tendring. The tracery, which is blind in these cases, is ascribed to *c.* 1350, and the profiles of the durns are shown in silhouette—these sections confirm the dating. What is of greatest interest is the fact that the dovetail joint is used, upside-down, to resist compression—as is shown at the right of the drawing. The object of this exercise was to give a firm standing to the wall pieces joined into the tops of the durns. At the present time the wall pieces carry hammer-beams and braces, but these appear to be a tie beam with its central length cut out. Fig. 80 shows the south door at Buttsbury which is cross-planked and rivetted, with ledges fitted between the planks on the back, or inside, face of the door. The Royal Commission dated the doorway to the 14th century, and the door must be of the same age. It is one of the few having grilled openings for the inspection of would-be entrants.

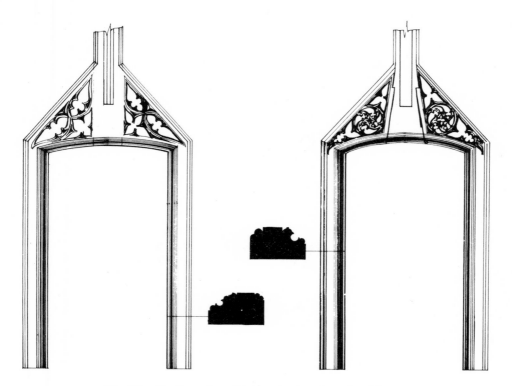

Fig. 79.   North and south door surrounds at Tendring

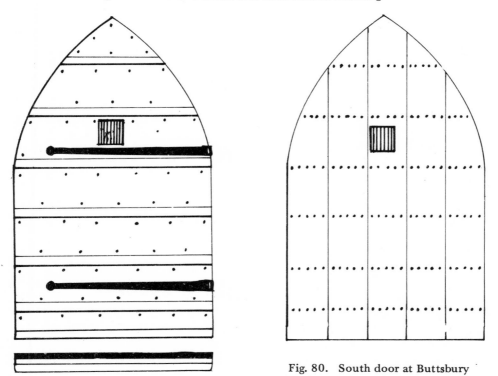

Fig. 80.   South door at Buttsbury

89

Six of the finest surviving doors of the Perpendicular period are illustrated next, beginning with the south door at Finchingfield which, as may be seen in Plate XXX, has been restored a little where necessary. This was ascribed by the Royal Commission to c. 1370. Tolleshunt D'Arcy possesses a finely framed south door which is shown in Fig. 81, very strongly built and well moulded, and is datable to between c. 1357 and c. 1400. The southern door at Great Bardfield is impressive, and it was dated by the Royal Commission to the late 14th century, as was its stone doorway. Both inner and outer faces are shown in Fig. 82. It is worthy of note that all expense was concentrated on its outer face, or front, and its rear frame saw no display of jointing. Fig. 83 shows both faces of the south door at Shalford which is evidently of the 14th century, and most probably of the middle decades. Like the preceding example, the expense was confined to the blind tracery of the outer face, and the rear frame was not, it appears, to be examined closely. Towards the close of the Perpendicular comes one pair of doors of superlative quality and restrained ornament, those at Salcott church which are illustrated in Fig. 84. Their carpentry is eclectic, since dovetail laps of both categories are used in addition to mortises and tenons. The four outside planks are carved with a single linenfold each, which is not terminated at the bottom rails. The two grown bends that form the heavy durns are good examples of their kind, and this door is ascribed to between c. 1500 and c. 1525.

The Anglo-Saxon door at Hadstock still swings on its original hinges; the frontal straps of these were apparently renewed during the 19th-century restoration, when it seems the originals, insofar as they were serviceable, were affixed to the west door of the tower. The carpentry of this door can give much valuable evidence, however, independently of its iron work. Firstly, its condition proves that the four planks forming the surfaces were seasoned timber at the time it was constructed, since no shrinkage can be found at the long joints between their edges. Had the timber been green, even to a slight extent, these joints would have opened as the planks became narrower, due to the shrinkage of their drying out. Secondly, it is evident that the principle of converting timber into 'quartered' plank, which is the most stable type of plank, was fully understood and practised at this early date. It is also indicated that the making of doors from selected and quartered timber was an aspect of a highly developed carpentering tradition as early as c. 1025.

These few facts are of importance and enable us to assess the remainder of these examples in relation to a dated first example, which is of a high standard of craftsmanship. The use of splayed rebates at the long edge joints is evidence for the use of a rebate plane, since these joints are very straight and close, and they would have been very difficult, if not impossible, to produce by any other tool or method. The rear frame indicates the use of either steam or heat bending; this is not too surprising as it has been necessary for shipbuilding since the earliest times. The use of the lozenge-shaped washers is also likely to derive from the iron clenches and roves, of similar shape, used earlier in the planking or straking of ships. The Buttsbury specimen is of the same period, being of identical manufacture, but it was re-used at least twice, the first occasion applying the Norman-style iron strapwork, and the second cutting it into a pointed arch.

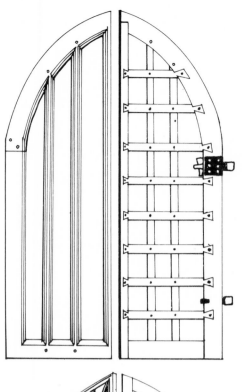

Fig. 81.   South doors at Tolleshunt D'Arcy
(Inset: stone moulding of door frame)

Fig. 82.   South doors at Great Bardfield

91

Fig. 83.   Door at Shalford

The doors illustrated in Figs. 68 and 69 have counter-rebated edges, of which type five examples are known in the county—three at Castle Hedingham, one at Elmstead Market, and one at Sutton, all of which appear to date from the later 12th century and the three examples at Hedingham are reconcilable with the general date of the fabric there, *c.* 1180. On small doors like those at Elmstead and Sutton the rebating is only triple, as shown in Fig. 69, but on massive doors like the southern one at

92

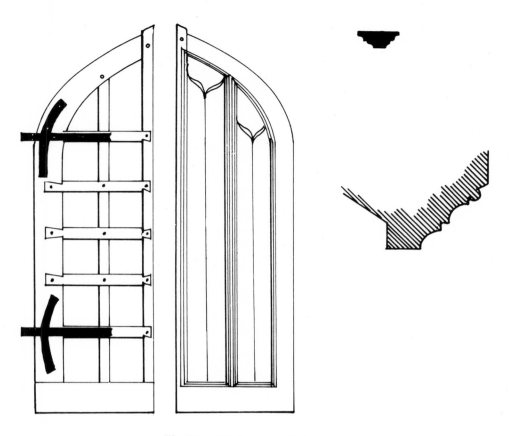

Fig. 84.   South door at Salcott
(Inset: stone moulding of door frame)

Hedingham the rebating seems unduly elaborate, and it is hard to explain this complexity. The planks available to the carpenter there were of inconsistent widths, and the rear face of the door has been covered by added planking so that neither framing, nor lack of it, can be seen.

The south door at Heybridge and the north door at Eastwood were both ascribed to the 12th century by the Royal Commission, but neither of them was counter-rebated and their iron work was far more elaborate. A way to reconcile these facts is to consider that the serpent-crescent type of irons culminated in the form shown in Fig. 72, and survives on the northern door at Eastwood. The timing of these developments within the 12th century would require an accurate iron-dating process, or at some future time dendrochronology may resolve the problem. It is obvious that the jointing of the southern door at Eastwood, and the highly sophisticated design of its tapered and dovetailed ledges together with the great width of its planks, tend to confirm a later dating than the counter-rebated specimens, and the 13th century is suggested. During this century very wide and well seasoned plank must have been available.

The White Roding door is of simpler carpentry, having only squared and butted edges, but the craft ethic of fixing its oaken planks and ledges together by means of fox-wedged pegs indicates the work of a more fastidious craftsman than was employed at Hadstock or Buttsbury. Notwithstanding the square edges this door was draught-proofed, since its abutments were covered over by strips of fullered iron spiked on each side of the joints. The foliated hinge irons may date during the Early English period, and the second half of the 13th century has been proposed regarding the nave roof of this church, but an earlier dating may later become possible. Other doors that may be Norman, if they are to be judged by their iron work, are those at Stifford and Wakes Colne, both having V-edged planking. If their dates could be proved to be Norman, then every type of edge jointing would have been known soon after the Conquest, and no developments, or few, could be proposed.

The south door at High Roding is apparently of the early 13th century and it is more a carpenter's artefact than the result of a smith-woodworker liaison. The construction is impressive, and evinces intelligent constructive thinking. The next two doors illustrated, those at Ashen and Little Leighs, are both distinctly Early English with foliated and visually plant-like iron work. The introduction at Ashen of V-edged planking in conjunction with fox-wedged pegging tends to place the inception of this planking method as late 13th century. The ultimate development of the iron work at Ashen is that retained on the largely renewed south door at Bocking.

The doors illustrated in Figs. 75, 76 and 77 show a wide diversity of treatment, so far as their rear frames are concerned, coupled with simple iron work, and all three were probably made during the first quarter of the 14th century. During the middle decades of the century the two door cases at Tendring were made with a view to supporting the wall pieces and braces fitted between their durns. A plain door of this century is the south door at Buttsbury, shown in Fig. 80. This is cross-boarded with ledges fitted between the inner boards, and the whole rivetted through.

The carved pair of doors shown in Plate XXX are those at Finchingfield, which were dated to c. 1370 by the Royal Commission. The rear frames are very well made and use lozenze-shaped washers and rivets, the ledges are halved under the vertical members, and pegging is used round the edge joints of the doors. The doors at Tolleshunt d'Arcy shown in Fig. 81 are of better quality, beautifully jointed and decorated with restrained mouldings of great depth. As a piece of well designed construction achieving the maximum of strength and elegance, the Tolleshunt doors must rank among the best of the Perpendicular period. The two pairs from Bardfield and Shalford both have finely carved outer faces that are fitted to the minimum of framing, indicating that the available finances were stretched a little beyond their limits, and that display was somewhat over-rated towards the end of this period. The illustrated examples conclude, however, with an excellent pair of centrally-divided doors from Salcott, shown in Fig. 84. They are as previously stated, eclectic, since the profusion of joint forms cannot be rationally explained; the second ledge from the bottom, for example, has a dovetailed lap at one end and a barefaced lap dovetail at the other—they are all good carpentry and well executed, but not justifiable.

Chapter Six

Gazetteer of Parishes*

Abberton, St. Andrew Nave roof of seven cants which has been plastered. Only one undatable tie-beam remains exposed.

Abbess Roding, St. Edmund Nave roof of seven cants, above tie beams set on wall pieces with traceried spandrels, the whole roof apparently dating from *c.* 1375–1400. The chancel roof is also framed in seven cants, above tie beams on wall pieces with steeply arched braces that have open spandrel voids — this should date from the Decorated period.

Abridge, Holy Trinity Brick church of the 19th century. Not visited.

Aldham, St. Margaret This church was rebuilt in 1855 by Hakewill, who was instructed to use again such timbers as were sound; details of this work are placed on view in the church. The south porch is of the 14th century, with much interesting tracery and S-curved braces to the collars, as is shown in Fig. 40. The nave roof is of 21 couples framed into seven cants without tie-beams. The chancel is also roofed in seven cants and with a few new rafters added at the restoration; the south aisle roof is very similar. It is evident that most timbers from all three roofs were retained, and there is some variety of mouldings among these separate sets of wall plate. An ogee-headed and cross-planked door was re-used at the time of the restoration, and now hangs in the south doorway of the tower as is shown in Fig. 77.

Alphamstone, of unknown dedication Nave roof in seven cants, and with evidently ancient timbers, showing no datable features. Both north and south doors are good and of uncertain age.

Alresford, of unknown dedication The quoins of both western corners date from the 13th century, the whole drastically restored in the 19th century. All that remains to be seen are one tie beam and one wall plate, possibly 14th century, in the nave. This church has now been reduced to a roofless ruin, due to a disastrous fire.

Althorne, St. Andrew Both nave and chancel roofs are Victorian and arched to the collars.

Ardleigh, St. Mary The roofs of the nave, chancel, and aisle are very poor quality, and result from a restoration. The south door, which the local information dates to 1460, is a good specimen and is richly traceried.

Arkesden, St. Mary Heavily restored in 1855.

Ashdon, All Saints Nave roof braced with trenched and tenoned scissors, the whole built in four bays and with tie beams. The chancel roof is remarkable in having down-braced crown posts, with foiling applied to the downward braces of the eastern post which is of keeled quatrefoil section, having four intervening fillets; apparently of *c.* 1325. This roof also has scissor braces of the trenched and tenoned variety, above the collar purlin. The south

*L.G.B.=Local Guide Book

chapel has a very similar roof, also scissored with collar purlin and crown posts of quatrefoil section—typologically of the early 14th century. The roofs to both north and south aisles are also of considerable interest.

Asheldham, St. Lawrence Not entered. Some unusual framing is visible at the eaves of the nave roof, on the southern side. Framed into seven cants so far as could be seen through the windows.

Ashen, St. Augustine of Canterbury The nave roof is plastered on its underside, leaving only the principal timbers visible; it is a remarkable roof which is arched to the collars. The south door is remarkable and is illustrated in Fig. 73.

Ashingdon, St. Andrew Nave roof of seven cants with crown posts, built in two bays. The chancel roof is arched to the collars with one side purlin each side.

Aythorpe Roding, St. Mary Nave roof framed in seven cants with tie beams, wall pieces and steeply-arched braces—all mouldings indicating the Perpendicular period. The belfry is mounted on the two western tie-beams, as shown in Fig. 57, and described on p. 66.

Bardfield Saling, St. Peter and St. Paul Nave roof of seven cants with four tie beams and plastered soffit. The chancel roof is also in seven cants with plastered soffit; its wall plates, however, are visible and date between *c.* 1340 and 1380, when the church was consecrated.

Barking, St. Margaret North porch with crown-post roof having a steeply cambered tie beam at the centre. The north aisle roof is built in nine bays with crown posts and seven cants, the eastern and western halves of this long roof are of different dates and characteristics. The central nave roof is camberbeamed and built in five bays, each beam resting on wall pieces, and each slope having two side purlins, the whole of Perpendicular date. A gateway also survives which now leads into the churchyard, which was formerly the Fire Bell Gate. It is of two storeys, the first floor being of nine joists that are lodged upon embedded side wall plates.

Barling, All Saints Nave roof of seven cants plastered over, and the chancel roof has deep wall pieces to its central frame; the north aisle has collars and side purlins obscured by a plastered soffit. The south porch is of timber, has double-ogee mouldings of the Perpendicular period and a central arch-braced tie beam of the late 15th century.

Barnston, of unknown dedication Both nave and chancel roofs have been obscured with plaster, and both are in seven cants. The nave has visible wall plates, cambered tie beams and wall pieces with arches braces. The bell turret is converted from medieval to something hardly recognisable—this would perhaps repay study.

Basildon, Holy Cross Chancel roof of seven cants with panelled, original finish. It is similar to the nearby chancel roof at Laindon which is shown in Plate X. The nave roof is a late example with side purlins clasped in collars, has five tie beams and is in four bays. The eastern gable is studded, above the collar. The south door is saltire-braced at its rear, and has four horizontal battens and nine V-edged boards. The tower has a good pair of west doors with portcullis frames. The south porch is a good specimen, timber-framed, and roofed in five cants. The mullions dividing the side lights are of double-ogee section, with slotted tops, for the support of tracery planks that are now missing. At the north tie beam there is a pair of four-centred, Tudor knees, which have interesting reliefs carved in their spandrels.

Beauchamp Roding, St. Edmund Nave roof with very tall crown posts, square in section, and having most unusual capitals and bases. They are braced to the collar purlin only. The roof is framed in seven cants and has been plastered; it must date from early in the 14th century. The chancel roof is also of seven cants, and with plastered soffit; it has a tie beam on wall pieces, and braces with void spandrels of Decorated aspect.

Beaumont-cum-moze, St. Leonard Of *c.* 1854, and by Hakewill. Examined.

Belchamp Otten, St. Ethelbert and All Saints South porch roofed in seven cants and with crenellated top plates. The chancel roof is also in seven cants with scissor braces made of tenoned short lengths; these are a type derived from the high-roof of Salisbury Cathedral's north-east transept, dated to *c.*1237. The nave roof is also in seven cants and there is a belfry at the west end, originally on portal frames. It is now carried by four eastern posts, the central pair of which are due to a 17th-century repair, and carved with 'guilloche' ornament. The turret was not examined.

Belchamp St. Paul, St. Andrew A south porch with timber roof in seven cants, it has crenellated wall plates similar to those in the chancel. The nave roof is also framed in seven cants and has composite scissors, made of tenoned short lengths; above the collars (see Fig. 35). The chancel roof is, again, in seven cants. It has double collars and most interesting wall plates which are illustrated in Fig. 35. The north aisle has two good Perpendicular roofs of differing ages.

Belchamp Walter, St. Mary Timber south porch with crown-post roof, good verge boards and plain, diagonal mullions without side tracery. 15th century. The very large and wide nave roof is of seven cants with plastered soffit; only three tie beams of poor quality timber are visible. The south door (see Fig. 76) is one of the most interesting, having a rear frame that is unique for this county—it is described on p. 86.

Berden, St. Nicholas The nave roof is of the 18th century, with king posts and raking struts; the collars were mortised on each face to carry ceiling joists that are now missing. This is similar to the nave roof at Bradwell-juxta-Mare. The roof of the south transept is of the late 15th century, according to the Royal Commission. It has a central hammerbeam truss with double collars, two side purlins in each slope, and two tiers of purlin wind bracing. This roof is unique in the county but is not illustrated.

Berechurch, St. Michael and All Angels The north chapel has a sumptuous hammer-beam roof of early 16th-century origin, which is discussed on p. 36, and illustrated in Plate VIII. The south door, made from fragments of linenfold panel and pieces of tracery repays a very close examination.

Berners Roding, of unknown dedication Nave roof with crown post and seven cants, possibly of the late 14th century. The chancel roof is of the Perpendicular period, and has Tudor details. It is also in seven cants with a short crown post.

Birch, St. Mary Of 1850, by Teulon. **Old St. Mary** A ruin, not examined.

Birchanger, St. Mary No timber of interest, or any age, is visible.

Birdbrook, St. Augustine of Canterbury An unusually fine nave roof in five bays, each having six common couples, it has collars with butted side purlins and arch braces from wall pieces to the collars which function as eave blades. The roof is not tied and is shown in Fig. 29, and described on p. 29.

Blackmore, St. Lawrence Nave roof in seven cants, panelled with bosses. It is a very high roof and difficult to examine. The belfry is one of the most impressive of its kind in England, and it is certainly the tallest in this county. This is more fully dealt with in the section on belfries and spires (Hewett, 1980, 201).

Black Notley, St. Peter and St. Paul. This church has an unusual belfry which is of 14th-century date, and is illustrated in Plate XXIV and described on p. 69. The south door is new and without any merit, but it carries some ironwork of the Norman period. The chancel roof is a good one framed in seven cants, with moulded wall plates and tie beam, dating by its mouldings to c. 1425-50.

Bobbingworth, St. Germain The nave roof is in seven cants and of three bays in length. The timbers are ancient but they are plain, and without any datable feature.

Bocking, St. Mary This church possesses a selection of very fine Perpendicular roofs, some of which may be datable within close limits if their decorative details are fully analysed. The north aisle, illustrated in Plate XIV and described under 'Roof Framing', is a fine specimen. The south door which has generally been ascribed to the 13th century has very elaborate, foliated ironwork on its outer face. This is illustrated in Plate XXIX, but owing to an unfortunate 'restoration' it has no rear framing and is reduced to a frontal surface.

Boreham, St. Andrew All the roofs are covered with plaster. The north aisle shows some principal timbers that are probably of the 17th century, while the timber porch is of the 15th century, and has ogee-and-hollow mullions.

Borley, of unknown dedication South porch of red brick with mitred wall plates and a segmental pointed arch, of timber, for the south doorway. The nave roof is one of the hybrids of types, having posts that are either king posts or crown posts, plastering rendering it impossible to determine which. These are mounted on the two intermediate frames and carry a collar purlin. At the east and west frames these posts stand upon tie beams, and the other two stand on the collars, which are supported by big timber arch braces. The chancel roof is of seven cants.

Bowers Gifford, St. Margaret The nave roof is ceiled and forms a four-centred arch; the tower contains a timber internal tower, that was not fully examined.

Boxted, St. Peter The nave roof, four bays long, is crown post and collar purlin with tall posts centrally, and short ones at each end that are corbel mounted. It is evidently of the 14th century, but is much obscured by plastering; nevertheless it is a very handsome example of its kind. The Norman west tower contains two archaic timber floors that could well be original. These are carried on joists which are, in turn, laid at right-angles across primary joists. The floors are thereby stiffened without the use of posts, braces, or framing.

98

Bradfield, St. Lawrence   All roofs of seven cants, without tie beams and ceiled; therefore un-examinable, but probably early in date.

Bradwell-juxta-Coggeshall, Holy Trinity   Timber south porch with scissor-braced and collarless roof, the side tracery and top-plate moulding indicating a 14th-century date. This example is illustrated in Fig. 38. The chancel roof is of seven cants with 14 couples closely spaced, and exposed to view, probably of the same date as the chancel itself. The nave roof has crown posts with collar purlin that were apparently fitted at the time, during the 14th century, when the eaves were raised, and the original roof of seven cants was re-used. The difference of surface patination is actually visible. The belfry is both rare and rewarding to view, having notch-lapped saltire braces in each wall. This example is illustrated and described in Fig. 54, and on p. 62.

Bradwell-juxta-Mare, St. Thomas   The south porch of this church is remarkable among its kind, having side-lights at its front half only; it is illustrated in Fig. 43, on p. 52. The nave roof is an example of Georgian carpentry with king posts and raking struts. Its tie beams are mortised for the joists of a ceiling which has not survived.

Braintree, St. Michael the Archangel   The nave roof is a good example with single hammerbeams and quatre-foil traceried spandrels in the voids of their arch braces; the clerestory was added (L.G.B.) in 1340 and the roof would, if the original, date from that time. It is, however, very lofty, and has not been examined at close quarters. The south aisle chapel has a very fine roof of six bays, richly decorated, and with closely datable late Perpendicular details. There is also a door of interest at the end of the north chapel; it is late Perpendicular and is locally ascribed to the 15th century (L.G.B.).

Brentwood, St. Thomas   By E. C. Lee and of 1882–90. Not examined.

Brightlingsea, All Saints   The west doors to the tower, which was begun late in the 15th century and was still uncompleted in 1548, are good. They were originally overlaid with pierced wooden tracery, of which a small fragment has survived. They are double doors with central shuts and portcullis framing at the rear. The south porch has a camber-beam roof with wall pieces, braced, and a ridge piece—all of the early 16th century. The nave roof is extremely poor, dating from after the collapse in 1814, and the subsequent restoration deprived the building of its clerestory. The north aisle is roofed in nine bays but only the principals are visible, which are of plain timber. The south aisle also shows only its principals through the plaster, but they are moulded. The tower has a good first floor framed on two pairs of crossing bridging joists. The latter are wall pieced all round, but unfortunately bungled at east and west owing to the existence of windows, or their later intrusion (L.G.B., C. R. Heard, 1944-59).

Broomfield, St. Mary   All the visible timber in this church seems to date from the restoration of 1870. The frame of the circular spire, however, is medieval and most rewarding.

Broxted, St. Mary   Much renovated, no timberwork noticed. The belfry looks both Victorian and spurious. Not ascended, however.

Bulmer, St. Andrew Has a very fine chancel roof, of the early 16th century, with arched braces to the collars and central pendants. The nave roof is also impressive, a 19th-century hammerbeam and side-purlin example with king posts above its collars—the whole wrought in resinous soft wood.

Bulphan, St. Mary This nave roof is ceiled, and invisible, but the south porch is uncommonly good. Illustrated in Fig. 50. The main feature is the western belfry, one of the most impressive type with posts aligned in an east-west colonnade. This is illustrated and described in Plate XXVIII, and on p. 69.

Burnham-on-Crouch, St. Mary Both north and south doors are interesting, one framed and the other, the southern one, cross-planked. No other timber in church.

Buttsbury, St. Mary The nave roof is known to be crown post but this was ceiled from view before the present examination. The chancel roof is still visible and is crown post with seven-canted common couples; this roof must have been retained when the 18th-century brick chancel was built. The roof of the north aisle is ancient and has carved oak corbels to its top wall plate. The south door is cross-planked and battened and is illustrated in Fig. 80. The north door is one of the most important in Essex, being of Anglo-Saxon construction, and is illustrated in Fig. 66.

Canewdon, St. Nicholas This church has a nave roof that is enigmatic in type, as the result of a restoration in 1908. It is basically an early crown-post roof with straight tie beams and seven cants, the crown posts being of quadrate section. Above the collars, however, are the remnants of scissor braces trenched into the rafters, and now terminating at their crossings. The west tower has a very good timber floor framed on diagonal bridging joists, in the manner commonly found in timber belfries. The tower is locally ascribed to Henry V, and his arms are carved therein, on stone. The south door is most unusual, being a pair with hinging down the central shuts, as well as at the harr. The planking is V-edged and the rear frame well wrought with seven battens, heavy edges of grown arcuation, and widely spaced verticals.

Castle Hedingham, St. Nicholas A magnificent nave roof, double hammerbeam, with numerous pendants. This is illustrated in Plate XV, and described under 'Roof Framing' on p. 37. A local tradition ascribed this roof to one Thomas Loveday who died in 1535, which date is acceptable for the structure and decoration. The chancel is roofed in seven cants and has evidently been restored. The south door is Norman, as is the north door. Both are remarkable for their great size and the complexity of their counter rebating. They are illustrated in Fig. 68. The south door in the chancel is also Norman, and these three are described on p. 80.

Chadwell St. Mary, St. Mary Not visited.

Chappel, St. Barnabas This church was consecrated as a chapel of ease to the church of Great Tey in 1352, and it became an independent parish in 1433. But so far as the age of the general fabric is concerned recent evidence indicates the existence of a chapel of Tey as early as 1285. The nave and chancel are continuous under a single roof, which is framed into seven cants and has no datable features; it is, however, probably as old as the general fabric. The small and square-spired belfry at the west end is apparently fully as old as the rest of the building, but has, unfortunately, been modified at some time past. At this time a pair of passing braces were shortened, after crossing the eastern posts, for no apparent reason. The south door and porch are unusual and probably of the early 17th century.

Chelmsford, St. Mary Not examined since much restored during recent years.

Chickney, St. Mary Chancel roof of seven cants, much modified, and a collar purlin has been added *above* its collars. The sole pieces lie on top of the wall plates, indicating a very early original date. The nave roof is crown post and seven cants built in two bays with a half bay at the western end— suggesting a belfry prior to the building of the tower. The three crown posts of the nave have double jowls and clasp the collar purlin, and the central post has capital and base treatment. The exact profile of the nave's central crown post has been recorded with a 'profile-comb', and it relates only to one example in Mr. S. E. Rigold's definitive work on 'Romanesque Bases in, and south-east of, the Limestone Belt' (S. E. Rigold, 1978, 109). This profile derives from multiple rolls, of which one towards the top is flattened. As Rigold observes, this form may be seen in the dorter-undercroft mélange at Canterbury, and a comparable date is probable. Part of a southern porch survives, of timber, which is of unusual character quite unlike the majority of its kind.

Chignal Smealey, St. Nicholas Nave roof arched to collars, and very well framed with well moulded wall plates and principal braces, of the early 16th century, as the church also is considered to date. The chancel roof is also of seven cants with its central frame arched to the collar. Its wall plates are differently moulded, but also of 16th-century character. Both north and south doors are of interest, that on the south being clearly Tudor with a four-centred head and heavy, portcullis-type, rear frame.

Chigwell, St. Mary The nave roof is of three bays, has quadrate sectioned crown posts and its collar purlin is framed onto the timber belfry at the western end. The belfry was reinforced by the addition of extra posts during either the late 16th, or the early 17th, century.

Chipping Ongar, St. Martin of Tours A church which has been described as an uncommonly complete Norman village church, and one that incorporates an astonishing variety of remnants of ancient timber roofs. The nave roof is a good specimen of crown posts, collar purlin and seven cants with tie-beam wall pieces having traceried spandrels. This is illustrated in Fig. 30, and described on p. 31.

The roof of the chancel is the most interesting, and incorporates the two most rare and ancient pieces of carpenters' method in the church. The whole roof, as it exists at the time of writing, was created in 1643—the date being carved on the central pendant. This dates only a side-purlin assembly onto which were laid various couples of rafters from earlier roofs, either 13th century or earlier. These are described on pp. 3-4 and illustrated in Fig. 3. The south aisle has an excellent lean-to roof with wall pieces and eaves-angle knees, the knees being carved with roses and leaves—of the 19th century.

Chrishall, Holy Trinity The roof to the north aisle is the only example of good carpentry—a lean-to roof with one purlin, rosettes at the purlin's junctions with the rafters; wall pieces and knees being carved with pomegranates and leaves. The local guide book ascribes this roof to *c*. 1420.

Little Clacton, St. James A document displayed inside this church gives dates for its main parts, apparently the result of some former incumbent's research. Of these dates, those for the south porch, 1381, and for the bell-turret, 1412, are of interest in this context. Both appear very feasible—the belfry is illustrated in Fig. 61, under that heading, and the porch is characteristically late 14th century. The nave roof is of seven cants and has suffered 'restoration'. Its ashlar pieces are nailed to the rafters' soffits, a fact that is in accord with the given date, 1346, in the church.

Clavering, St. Mary and St. Clement Perpendicular clerestory carrying a good camber-beam roof of the same period.

Colchester, All Saints Now used as a museum annexe. Nave and chancel roofed in seven cants. North aisle with slightly pitched well-timbered roof, its members moulded in the manner of the late 16th century. The north door is good early Perpendicular.

Holy Trinity Derelict at time of writing. South porch roofed with five couples of seven cants. South door of Decorated shape, strap-hinged V-edged boarded. South aisle, east, arched to collars. Aisle and central chancel of seven cants with tie beam at its centre.

St. Martin Nave roof in seven cants, with tenoned joints, as are the north and south aisles, and their transepts. The three tie beams across the nave have roll-moulded corners, perhaps of the 14th century. The chancel has a most impressive 14th-century roof with elaborate crown post, at the central frame. This has a steeply cambered tie beam with traceried spandrels to its arch braces of good and large quatrefoiled character. The soffit of this roof is framed into an arch by the use of curved collar braces and ashlar pieces. The church is now de-consecrated and serves as a theatre.

Cold Norton, St. Stephen Built in 1855 by Pritchett. Not examined.

Colne Engaine, St. Andrew South porch with crown-post roof on red brick walls. Nave roof of early crown-post design with downward bracing laterally from posts to tie beams. One of the better 14th-century examples. Chancel roof arched to collars and apparently much restored.

Copford, St. Mary the Virgin An all-Norman church with scissored nave roof, and this roof seems of characteristically late 13th-century construction, having tenoned end joints to its scissors. The roof is extremely high, well above the springing of the original vaults, and cannot be examined until receiving major repairs. In the west bay is a timber belfry standing on two very tall posts, with arched braces and a transom from north to south. Belfry not examined owing to its height and absence of ladders.

Corringham, St. Mary Of structural carpentry the only visible item is the wall plate of the north aisle. This is crenellated and hollow-moulded, and could be of the 14th century.

Cressing, All Saints The chancel is in seven cants with crenellated wall plates, and of uncertain date. The nave roof is most unusual, as it has tie beams set on wall pieces and arched braces. It is arched above these to its collars and has side purlins with tracery between the collar arches and principal rafters. Above the collars are crown posts, collar purlin and seven cants. This doubtless important essay in roof framing is illustrated in Fig. 27, and described on p. 28. There is a western belfry built upon two portal frames and with bracing of distinctly Tudor arcuation, which is discussed on p. 76.

Dagenham, St. Peter and St. Paul The chancel roof is of seven equal cants. Its underside is plastered over. The north aisle has a similar roof, equally obscured.

Danbury, St. John the Baptist The north aisle has a rare example of timber roofing, with every common-rafter couple framed into an arch. This is contrived by the fitting of four 'compassed' timbers which are chase-tenoned to the collars and rafters. The roof is illustrated in Fig. 10, and described on pp. 12-13. This roof is apparently the original one for the north aisle, but has later additions, such as the ribs and panelling with carved head corbels of *c.* 1412.

   The nave roof is of equal interest and a local record testifies that it was 're-built', after sustaining severe damage in a tempest, in 1402. The same record states that the chancel roof also received attention at this time. What in fact appears to have occurred in the nave is a re-use of its early 13th-century, scissor-braced roof, combined with crown posts, and central purlin, the difference in surface patina of the respective timbers being clearly visible. The existing chancel roof is of trussed rafters in seven cants, and with a 15th-century wall plate. The south aisle is problematical in that it closely reproduces that over the north aisle, but its curvature is different and it is unlikely to be of equal age.

Debden, St. Mary the Virgin and All Saints This church has no visible timber, but the elaborate roof of the Chiswell chapel at its eastern end is framed in timber, plastered, and dated to 1793.

Dengie, St. James Nave roof of seven cants, with rafters' feet on top of its sole pieces — an indication, generally, of early date.

Doddinghurst, All Saints The south porch is of unusual length, built in two bays. This is illustrated in Fig. 51. The nave roof is unique in having alternate double and single collars, combined with high king posts and a ridge piece. The whole is crown post, and framed in two bays. This roof is illustrated in Fig. 20, and described on p. 22.

Dovercourt, All Saints A rare nave roof with crown posts constituting a very early example of their type, and having 'crown' capitals, resulting from the application of crenellation to the octagon. These are mounted on tie beams having wall pieces (buried under the plaster) and arched braces with void spandrels, the whole being of the mid-14th century. This roof is illustrated in Fig. 21, and has double, clasping collars at its half-bay intervals. The rood beam at the chancel division bears a 17th-century date and carved volutes. See Plate XVII.

Downham, St. Margaret Timber south porch of the 15th century. The red brick tower formerly contained some extremely fine bell frames and wheels, of the early 16th century, as was its pyramid roof. Most of this has been destroyed recently.

Earls Colne, St. Andrew The roof to the south aisle probably dates from *c.* 1360 when the de Vere family, Earls of Oxford, inaugurated some improvements. The south porch was also built by the de Veres, in *c.* 1460. The handsome west tower, built between 1460 and 1534, has a fine first floor on two bridging joists each way and crossing centrally. All have wall pieces with open voided arch braces.

East Ham, St. Mary Magdalene Containing an apsidal roof at the east end, this is illustrated and described on page 8. The chancel has a crown-post roof which has evidently been 'restored', and the nave roof is of seven bays with raised ties and canted ashlar pieces.

East Hanningfield, All Saints In ruins 1953-54. Not examined.

East Horndon, All Saints Not examined.

East Mersea, St. Edmund King and Martyr Nave and chancel roofs both framed in seven cants, and plastered, their wall-plate sections suggesting the close of the 15th century.

Easthorpe, St. Mary the Virgin Roof modern.

East Tilbury, St. Catherine Both nave and north aisle roofs result from a 'restoration'. Chancel roof of seven cants with four tie beams. The north door has V-edged planks, but a renewed rear frame.

Eastwood, St. Laurence and All Saints The north and south doors are of great importance and they are dealt with on pp. 81-2. The nave roof is crown post with collar purlin and seven cants, and this is described on page 18. The chancel roof is in three bays of four common rafters each. Timber tower with spire, set upon a short stone base. This was not closely examined, but carries two bells and is of obvious interest. The bells are by William Burford, and of the 14th century. The north aisle contains a timber-framed partition, apparently of the 15th century, and forming a priest's room at the west end.

Elmdon, St. Nicholas Victorian, with the exception of the west tower.

Elmstead Market, St. Ann and St. Laurence The north door is illustrated in Fig. 69, and it is of the counter-rebated type. The south door has filleted joints with five rear battens, and is of Decorated arcuation. Some early moulded roof timbers are visible.

Elsenham, Dedication not known Nave with a crown-post roof in five bays. The collar purlin has a through-splayed scarf and the rafters have double collars. Not later than early 14th century.

Epping Upland, All Saints South door of cross-planked construction with strap hinges and rebated rear planks; the head arch is four-centred and the whole of *c.* 1450. The south porch is of similar date with a crown-post roof in two bays (central post of cross-quadrate section), trenched collars and diagonally-set mullions in the four side openings, which have no tracery.

Fairstead, St. Mary Both nave and chancel are usually considered to be Norman, with Roman brick dressings; some disturbance is visible below the eaves, externally, and the existing roof of seven cants has been raised, leaving three original tie beams *in situ* under the later ones. The oldest tie beams have unusually stop-chamfered soffits, and may date close to the Conquest. The west tower is considered to be of the 13th century, and contains an interesting contemporary first floor and a good timber spire.

Farnham, St. Mary the Virgin 1859, by Joseph Clarke.

Faulkbourne, St. Germanus Nave roof with tall crown posts that seem to be intrusions, but may be copies of the originals. This roof was of three bays and has had its western tie beam cut out at some time. The south door is framed into an oaken case that mounts a wall piece for the western tie beam, which is beneath the east end of the belfry. The south door is of late Decorated shape and is built upon a heavy rear frame of very good quality carpentry. Belfry not ascended.

Feering, All Saints The nave roof is of great interest, and is shown in Plate XIX. It has two side purlins each slope, with alternate braced collars and tie beams. The chancel roof is a contemporary copy of the 14th-century original—now gone. The south door is not illustrated and it is of uncertain date.

Felsted, Holy Cross The west tower was built in the decade 1120–30, and contains inside a timber tower which is of late 13th-century date, typologically, and has a notched lap joint cut upon one of its upright posts, perhaps indicating a second use of some earlier timbers. To the south is a chapel built by Lord Riche, in accordance with his father's will which was proved in 1582. This has a roof of 21 couples having arched braces to their collars. The chancel roof is of seven cants with wall plates showing three-quarter hollow mouldings, apparently of the 14th century (L.G.B., M. Craze, 1969).

Finchingfield, St. John The nave roof is of the camberbeam type with wall pieces. It is inscribed at its eastern end: '1561, W.B.S.L.'. The chancel roof is of similar date and type. To the north of the chancel is the Kempe Chapel dating from the late 14th century. This chapel has an extremely fine crown-post roof with uncommonly moulded timbers. The south door is in two halves, and of *c.* 1370. This is shown in Plate XXX. The screen is one of the most elaborate.

Fingringhoe, St. Ouen, now St. Andrew This church has a remarkable nave roof, of which type there are only two in the county, the other being at Thorpe-le-Soken. It is round arched to the collars, which are double and clasp the collar purlin. It has diagonal spurs projecting inward from its rafters and clasping the arched braces, the inner ends of which are carved with good portrait studies. These are all shown in Plate III. The chancel roof is very similar but less well adorned. The south door is very well framed and traceried and of the late 14th century.

Fobbing, St. Michael A nave roof of four bays with straight tie beams on wall pieces, crown posts and seven cants. The north aisle roof is also of four bays with three tie beams on similar wall pieces and arch braces having traceried spandrels—the tracery is of poor quality but stylistically pertaining to the close of the 14th century. Above the tie beams are crown posts (quadrate) and seven cants. The two end frames, east and west, are arched to the collars from deep wall pieces and have high crown posts upon their lower collars. The north chancel roof is of seven cants with three frames massively arched to their collars from wall pieces, possibly of the late 14th century. The south chapel roof is of 13 couples framed in seven cants. The west tower has a good first floor with hollow-moulded timbers that are probably as old as the tower. Both north and south doors are of unusual interest and unusually early date.

Ford End, St. John the Evangelist 1871, by Chancellor.

Fordham, All Saints A church with many roofs, all of which are ceiled and un-examinable.

Foulness, St. Mary the Virgin 1840, by Wm. Hambley. Not visited.

Foxearth, St. Peter and St. Paul A nave roof of great interest, arched from wall pieces to raised ties with diagonal, butted spurs, and collars above framed into seven cants. The whole roof is four bays long, and is shown in Fig. 12, and described on p. 14. The chancel roof is a single hammerbeam example with angels on the hammers, the whole magnificently painted and gilded, perhaps during the restoration of 1885 by J. Clarke. Both roofs may be of *c.* 1340, which is the possible date for both chancel fabric and north arcade. (Sir N. Pevsner, 1954, 168).

Frating, Dedication not known All the carpentry appears to date from some 19th-century rebuilding, but the south porch is a very impressive example, illustrated in Fig. 39, and of the 14th century.

Fryerning, St. Mary No visible carpentry of age or merit.

Fyfield, St. Nicholas All visible carpentry of the 19th century.

Gestingthorpe, St. Mary The west door to the tower seems contemporary with the tower, *c.* 1500. The nave roof is one of the most impressive in the county, double hammerbeams and dated 1489 by inscription. Shown in Plate IX, and described on p. 37. South porch of similar date to the tower, and with king-post roof of eight couples. The south door is good with linenfold planks that lack terminals; the 'folds' may have been planed on, framed on two durns, three stiles and five dovetailed ledges.

Goldhanger, St.Peter A crown-post nave roof with collar purlin and seven cants. This roof is illustrated in Fig. 18, and described on p. 21, and would seem to date from 1375–1400 in view of the various mouldings shown in the figure. The south aisle roof is difficult to date, and is arched to the collars.

Good Easter, St. Andrew The nave roof is of pine, arched to its collars, and of the 19th century. There is a reproduction belfry in the west end which stands on four posts, and the chancel roof may incorporate some early components; c.f. its south wall plate.

Gosfield, St. Catherine Nave roof arched to collars which clasp the principal rafters; the arches are also clasped by the spur ties. This roof is illustrated in Figure 25, and fully described on pages 26-27. This roof dates from *c.* 1435, when a major renovation occurred. A screen-like frame dividing the western bay of the nave from the rest may have been associated with a timber bell turret. The south doors are a pair with central shuts and traceried fronts of rich character, and their rear framing is lap jointed. Some late 16th-century timbers can be seen in the north chancel chapel.

Grays Thurrock, St. Peter and St. Paul　All visible carpentry of 1846.

Great Baddow, St. Mary the Virgin　Camberbeamed nave roof of *c*. 1510, with folded leaf decoration on the principals and carved wall-piece finials. North aisle has an unusual canted roof having tie beams and raking struts which support a central purlin. The tie beams are mounted on jowled wall posts.

Great Bardfield, St. Mary the Virgin　Nave roof of seven cants with tie beams on wall pieces. North and south aisles also have good roofs with knees and wall pieces, corbels, etc. The chancel roof, of seven cants, is dated *c*. 1618, from records concerning its donor—Edward Bendlowes. South door with lap-jointed rear frame and richly traceried front, having much ogee reticulation which is shown in Fig. 82.

Great Bentley, St. Mary the Virgin　Nave roof arched to its collars, by means of composite arches, possibly of *c*. 1500, but its date is not certain; the common couples are framed into seven cants. The chancel roof is also in seven cants with wall plates dating from 1475–1500. These chancel rafters change in patina at the point indicating the former existence of an apsidal east end, which has been squared. The south door is Norman, but of no particular merit.

Great Braxted, All Saints　The timber south porch has a crown post and crenellated ties. The chancel is roofed in seven cants and plastered over; its wall plates are very long, however, and show a good scarf joint half way along their length—of the 14th century. The north transept has a very good roof dated 1761, and commemorating a du Cane, of local importance.

Great Bromley, St. George　Nave roof double hammerbeams with arcading between its wall pieces. This is built in eight frames, with four intervening couples, ridge piece on king pieces above collars. North aisle roof good, of early Perpendicular style. North and south doors both good.

Great Burstead, St. Mary Magdalene　Nave and chancel with south aisle and chancel, comprising four separate timber roofs, north chancel of two bays, crown post and seven cants with rafters looking older than the crown posts—? posts inserted beneath an earlier roof of seven cants. Nave roof, four bays, three tie beams and two half-sectioned end ties; crown post and seven cants, rafters and cants look older than post system, which seems Perpendicular. The nave ties are all either straight or sagging and have only five couples between them. East end of south aisle has a crown-post roof of two bays, with crenellated tie beams on wall pieces having solid knees with carved faces. The collar purlin at the east end rests on a short post standing on a stone corbel, carved with England and France quarterly, possibly *c*. 1412. The rafters look earlier than the post system. South aisle, four bay roof of quadrate crown post and collar purlin, with straight and chamfered tie beams, five couples per bay. All four roofs of uncertain dates.

North and south doors both interesting, framed with barefaced dovetails.

North porch of timber, good, of 15th century. Two bays, crown post. South porch with crown-post roof of seven couples; oddly late and very flat heads to the side lights which may be of *c*. 1600–25.

Great Canfield, St. Mary Nave and chancel roofs of seven cants, and both with inclined ashlar pieces, the chancel has double collars. Dates of both are uncertain. Western timber belfry of rather slight framing, but considerable height, and with interesting turret and spire seating.

Great Chesterford, All Saints Nave roof Perpendicular, straight tie beams with short king posts, wall pieces and knees. The chancel roof is extremely similar, typologically the same. The south aisle has at its western end an unusually fine roof. The north aisle also has a good roof which is plainer.

Great Clacton, St. John the Baptist Norman church with nave and chancel that were originally vaulted, and are now roofed with seven cants, too high for inspection. A timber bell turret survives, between western tie beams and the pitches of the roof; this must date from some time prior to the existing stone tower of the 15th century.

Great Coggeshall, St. Peter-ad-Vincula Very severely damaged by enemy action in World War II. Some timbers in the nave and chancel roofs are evidently of Perpendicular period origin. Not examined, owing to great height above floor.

Great Dunmow, Dedication not known The chancel was under repair when seen (1970), and was of seven cants with inclined ashlar pieces, probably mid-14th century, as is chancel fabric. Nave roof interesting but of little merit. The aisles, both north and south, have good quality canted roofs of Perpendicular period. South door good and of early arcuation, with central 'shuts' and 10 dovetailed bars at rear and hollow mouldings on its front. Fine first floor in the west tower having two pairs of crossed bridging joists carved with heraldry at their crossings.

Great Easton, St. John and St. Giles No ancient timbers visible.

Great Hallingbury, St. Giles All but west tower and chancel arch are of 1874, it is alleged. Not visited.

Great Henny, St. Mary Nave roof with alternate tie beams and arch-braced collar frames, both with wall pieces, arch braces and side purlins, see Fig. 33. Described on p. 34. All arcuation in this roof is distinctly Tudor. The wall pieces have carved musicians, possibly of mid-15th century. South porch is brick with king-post roof, set on very wide wall plates.

Great Holland, All Saints All but west tower by Blomfield, of 1866.

Great Horkesley, All Saints South porch a very good example, probably of 1450-1500, with cinquefoil side tracery. The nave roof is an important example, arched to the collars with the collar purlin tenoned into the principal collars. This is illustrated in Fig. 32; the wall-plate mouldings suggest the mid-15th century. The second wall piece from the chancel arch on the north side is carved with a kneeling figure. Chancel roof similarly arched to its collars, but having the addition of a diagonally orientated pendant under the bay, and half-bay, collars.

Great Leighs, St. Mary Very early round tower base, locked, could contain early joists. The chancel roof is a copy, apparently of 1866 (L.G.B.), having tenoned scissor braces and collars—seven cants.

108

Great Maplestead, St. Giles Only the roof to the apse appears to have survived the last, and far-reaching, renovation, so it is most unlikely to be earlier than 15th century. The west tower, the base of which is Norman, has interesting but not original floors and bell frames.

Great Parndon, St. Mary I am indebted to A. V. B. Gibson of Bishop's Stortford for this report. Nave roof converted, crudely, into a single hammerbeam, with wall pieces occasionally pendant before window openings. The outer wall plate looks genuine Perpendicular.

Great Saling, St. James the Great Chancel roof of seven cants, having an inner wall plate with carved fleurons in a hollow moulding, now painted red and gold. The date of this is uncertain, but if a copy was made during the 1857–64 renovation it may well be accurate. No other 'fleuron' wall plate seen in this county. Nave with Victorian hammerbeams in pine, and south porch roofed in five cants, with apparently Perpendicular wall plates.

Great Sampford, St. Michael Nave roof in four bays of seven cants with tie beams having no wall pieces. Much of the general fabric is ascribed to the early 14th century. Chancel also roofed in seven cants, and having an inner wall plate of 14th-century section. The north aisle roof is a good lean-to, see Fig. 11, with compassed ashlar pieces and the same 14th-century style of wall plate as the chancel. The south (Lady) chapel is of the 13th century and is roofed with 12 couples of tenoned scissor braces and collars, steeply pitched. The south door is also of great interest, having an elaborately saltire-braced rear frame, see Fig. 78.

Great Stambridge, St. Mary and All Saints North porch of timber, and of interest; with tie beam and wall-plate sections indicative of late 15th century. The roof is crown post, and the side-light mullions set diagonally, while the door-way posts are curiously mitred at their top ends, to meet the tie beam.

Great Tey, St. Barnabas Chancel roofed in seven (plastered) cants, apparently of 14th century, as is the fabric of that part. West tower Norman with much interesting carpentry: the central newel stair has an oaken newelpost, scarfed and embedded in masonry. The roof is slightly pitched, and appears to be as old as the tower or nearly as old. The floor of the bell chamber is elaborate incorporating four joist joints and datable only by the most recent of them. The surviving piece of a south aisle has a low-pitched lean-to roof of the 14th century, good quality but difficult to view.

Great Totham, St. Peter Bell-turret lights fitted with fine and logically datable traceries of thick oak—two cinquefoiled lights per face. Inside this turret everything gutted out and renewed. Nave roof of seven cants above tie beams with wall pieces and knees. It is plastered between the ashlar pieces, and this plastering is probably original, as it evidently was in many instances. Chancel roof of seven cants, panelled, with north wall plate of *c.* 1475.

Great Wakering, St. Nicholas Nave roof of three bays with octagonal crown posts, collar purlin and seven cants; tie beams wall-pieced and arch-braced beneath. South door with a very curious partly saltire-braced rear frame and roll-moulded face on its planks.

Great Waltham, St. Mary and St. Lawrence South porch with Perpendicular camber-beam roof having typically numerous roll mouldings of the 16th century. West tower, originally Norman, has a timber tower frame inside which rises to the first floor. This is of uncertain date and has its upper reaches removed. Probably very late 13th century. Impressive nave roof of alternate tie beams with wall pieces, and single hammerbeams; this is, unfortunately, plastered everywhere between its main timbers. The chancel roof seems mainly 19th century. There is a good, small door of Decorated arcuation.

Great Warley, St. Mary the Virgin 1904 by Harrison Townsend.

Great Warley, Christ Church 1855, by Teulon. Tower only.

Great Wigborough, St. Stephen Nave roof has a good Victorian hammerbeam system, the chancel has collars with V-struts above, also Victorian, as is the porch.

Great Yeldham, St. Andrew South door good with V-edged boards and interesting rear frame. Doors to south porch very good workmanship of Perpendicular character and arcuation.

Greensted, St. Andrew Victorian.

Greensted-juxta-Ongar, St. Andrew The justly famous nave is built, as described on pp. 1-2, of oak trunks split into two halves and reared with their cambium outwards, set on a sill and tenoned into a top plate. The *method* of fitting the two top plates, with tie beams between them, appears to have survived the rebuilding of the 19th century, but the centre of the west gable was either destroyed, or entered private collections, at that time. The west tower has been examined, it incorporates no ancient timbers, and must date from the 18th century since an engraving of 1748 (E.R.O., Mint Portfolio) shows the entire west end with a narrow doorway and no tower.

Hadleigh, St. James the Less All roofs were replaced after heavy damage during World War II. Not examined.

Hadstock, St. Botolph There are some grounds to assume that this may be Cnut's minster, consecrated in 1016 (Hart, 1971, 1-12). The north door is accepted as Anglo-Saxon, and is shown in Fig. 65, and fully described under the heading of 'Doors'. The windows of the nave have oaken frames which are also original, and of the early 11th century (Hewett, 1980, 23). Quite unknown is the roof of the nave—which is shown in Fig. 2. Built in five bays with four tie beams which have survived, but in such infirm condition that later beams have been laid over them to support the roof. The whole was boarded over and clad with lead until 1725, at which date the metal was sold and a lighter cladding fitted, in the form of slates.

The king posts were designed to support the ridge piece which is pentagonal, and mortised for the rafters' upper ends: the posts were therefore compressed and the ties supported the roof as a dead weight. The principal rafters were given a T-section above the queen posts and the collars fitted at each half-way bay were very slightly cambered. The ridge piece is so broken, decrepit, repaired and fished that its original scarfing is difficult to assess, but one long through-splayed scarf does exist, secured with iron spikes. All the original timbers are square in section, and where waney edges occur the tenons' shoulders are scribed to meet them. The eaves catches are long, and fitted in the manner shown. One of its king posts was carbon[14] dated by the British Museum, 11 August 1972, and gave the result: BM-714. 499 ± 46 B.P. (*c.* 1451).

Halstead, St. Andrew The chancel roof was examined during recent repairs, when it was seen that a 19th-century inner surface was fitted to the early roof, which was specified in an Agreement between a carpenter and St. Paul's (L. F. Salzman, 1952, 490), dated 1413. The original 'ribs' of this·still protrude on the archivolt, and are coloured and gilded.

Harlow, St. Mary the Virgin Heavily restored 1878-80. One late Norman window survives at the north-west. The plan is cruciform, with crossing tower and a large brooch spire that has not been ascended.

Harlowbury, Chapel Desecrated for some centuries, and some time converted to granary uses. It has in the past been dated to *c.* 1180 by its carved capitals on the shafts of the north doorway — set in the 'nooks' of two square orders. This is illustrated and described elsewhere (C. A. Hewett, 1980, 47-8). It was re-roofed sometime soon after *c.* 1300, and this roof replaced the original, which was mounted upon pitched wall tops, without level string courses — as was the helm at Sompting and St. Martin's church in Canterbury. Work during the 'Saxo-Norman overlap' is implied by these facts. The existing roof has crown posts with late examples of the carinated fillet on their capitals, and an unusual scarf in its collar purlin. Embedded, mid-wall, in the gables are contemporary rafter couples that have halved collars and apexes, in contra-distinction to the later couples. The original rafters were also embedded in the inclined upper facets of the walls.

Harwich, St. Nicholas 1821 by M. G. Thompson.

Hatfield Broadoak, St. Mary the Virgin South door formerly good, but restored. North and south aisle roofs good.

Hatfield Peverel, St. Andrew The nave is that of the former Benedictine priory and is roofed with six principal frames that are arched to their collars. These rest on stone corbels by means of wall pieces. The eastern frame, at the chancel division, has a tie beam with arch braces beneath it of very flat Tudor arcuation. There are seven couples per bay, of renewed common-rafters. North door, double with central shuts, good, and heavy rear frame assembled with barefaced dovetails.

Havering-atte-Bower, St. John the Evangelist 1875–8, by Basil Champneys.

Hawkwell, St. Mary Nave roof is crown post (octagonal with capitals and bases), and collar purlin with seven cants. Tie beams are cambered and the inner wall plates tenon into their flanks. Western belfry of timber which is very directly framed and stands on only four posts of simple sections. The arch braces suggest an early Perpendicular date. (Turret not examined.) South door with two pairs of saltire braces at the rear and V-edged planks, assembled with return nails. Date uncertain but at least as early as the 15th century (RCHM).

Helion Bumpstead, St. Andrew Chancel roof of seven cants, plastered, and un-examinable. Nave roof interesting and formed into a four-centred arch that is plastered. No visible roof timber. North door, cross-planked and strap-hinged. Chancel door, south, good.

Hempstead, St. Andrew Chancel roof of seven cants, 15 couples, and with wall plates scroll-and-bead moulded; possibly late 14th century. North door quite good with double-hollow reeds on front. Some old knees re-used in the south porch are carved with armorial bearings which must be datable.

Henham, St. Mary the Virgin The nave roof was heavily reinforced at the beginning of the century, but retains its ancient frames above the intruded timbers. It is of four bays with four tie beams and with scissor braces that cross its collars; the end joints of these scissors cannot be seen owing to the presence of an inserted side purlin — but if notch-lapped would question the date of the general fabric, which does incorporate some early Romanesque stones. The south door is early Perpendicular in shape, and has an interesting rear frame.

Heybridge, St. Andrew South porch of almost contemporary workmanship, but incorporating a central tie beam of 14th-century character. South door Norman and with a complete set of encrusting ironwork. See Fig. 70. The nave roof has four tie beams and crown posts, five couples per bay, and both interior and outer wall plates without sole pieces. Three of the tie beams have wall pieces with knees in their angles; these are carved with monograms which are datable. I am much indebted to Mr. J. McCann for the information that this work is documented to 1517 or 1518, in *The Reformation in Essex*, by J. E. Oxley (pp. 28–9). Chancel roof in two bays with two quadrate crown posts and seven cants, terminating in a single hammerbeam frame at the east window.

High Beech, Holy Innocents 1873 by Sir A. Blomfield.

High Easter, St. Mary the Virgin The clerestory is covered by one of the most important roofs in Essex from the historical point of view. The north spandrel of the third tie beam from the west end is carved with a gate — an heraldic device associated with the Gate family, connected with both Garnetts and Merks. Sir Geoffrey Gate died in 1525, and appears to have left funds for the purpose of building clerestory and roof at some later date. The pitch is low, and short queen posts surmount the beams; there is pierced-plank arcading between the beams, and curved over the window heads. The pierced ornaments bear little relationship to any Gothic ones, and the actual date may be *c.* 1600 or even later. This is illustrated in Plate XVI. The chancel roof appears to be of the 19th century, and the south door is Norman, with original boards and strap hinges — one rear ledge survives with iron roves and clenches.

High Laver, All Saints Nave roof of three bays framed in seven cants, tie beams well cambered and wall plates with three-quarter hollow moulding of the 14th century. Chancel roof of three bays with two tie beams surmounted by seven cants, wall plates of Perpendicular profile and uncertain date. The west tower is surmounted by a recessed spire — not examined. South door of either late Decorated or early Perpendicular arcuation, and its rear frame assembled with square lap joints.

112

High Ongar, St. Mary The chancel is roofed in seven cants and has wall plates with characteristically Perpendicular mouldings—possibly of 1400–50. The nave has five tie beams with straight soffits and a slight camber to their upper faces. The crown posts are octagonal in section and have the bell-shaped spread at the foot which characterises the Perpendicular period.

High Roding, All Saints Nave roof with four bays framed in seven cants with double collars. Its wall plates have mouldings which emphasize sections of the circle, and include a small bowtell within the largest hollow which suggests 1350–1400. This roof is shown in Fig. 19, on p. 22. The chancel has a central tie-beam on wall pieces and 18 couples framed into seven cants, and the tie beam and wall-plate sections indicate the Perpendicular period. The south door (see Fig. 72) is of great interest, dating from the 13th century.

Hockley, St. Peter Nave roof in three bays with straight tie beams and crown posts of square section that have unusually simple capital and base treatment. The rafters are framed in seven cants and have double collars. The jointing of the sole piece and ashlars is also unusual (see Fig. 13). The wall plates are hollow moulded and of the 14th century. The west tower has a timber, four-post structure within of considerable interest; it is surmounted by a recessed spire which was not examined.

Horndon-on-the-Hill, St. Peter and St. Paul South porch of timber with an interesting roof construction that is arched to the collars, and has spur ties at eaves level, and a collar purlin. Chancel roof of seven cants, with hollow chamfered tie beams (Perpendicular). The Nave roof is crown post and collar purlin with seven cants, the tie beams are straight and its date uncertain, since no mouldings exist. The dormer windows in the nave are intrusions (see truncated ashlar pieces) and may be of the 16th century. Both north and south aisles have interesting roofs, that of the south aisle being in *three cants*—a rare feature in lean-to roofing.

Hutton, All Saints Chancel roof appears to be Victorian, good nave roof with quadrate section crown posts, and braces of Decorated arcuation. Since the arcades are 14th-century this roof could be of similar age. It is, however, high and dark, rendering examination difficult. The western belfry is a very interesting example. The north porch is of timber with six couples having trenched collars; the side-light traceries are of Perpendicular character.

Hythe, St. Leonard Nave roof is single hammerbeam without pendants, a very good specimen. The chancel roof is arched to the collars, from wall pieces, and has half-bay angel corbels. The roof to the north aisle is a very good one, slightly inclined with wall pieces and knees—probably Perpendicular. South door is double with central shuts and V-edged boards, good knocker, but a new rear frame.

Ilford Five churches, either of the 19th or 20th centuries.

Ingatestone, St. Edmund and St. Mary Nave roof with three tie beams, crown posts, collar purlin and seven cants. The collar purlin is joined (not scarfed) on the top of a crown post, the two ends butting and jointly forming a mortise, with two edge pegs each. The date of this roof could well be very early, and the wall plates, internally, are double and have double hollow mouldings. There are no sole pieces proper, but short ties placed behind each ashlar-piece tenon into both inner, and outer, wall plates. The chancel roof is also of seven cants, as is the south aisle roof, which has been restored. The south chancel has an interesting two-bay roof with side purlins which is dated to 1556 (L.G.B.). It has a cambered central tie beam and is framed in seven cants beneath its collars, and it is unsystematically wind-braced above the side purlins. The internal, and outer, wall plates are framed together with six keys per bay, and the outer plate shows a long example of the edge-halved and bridle-butted scarf.

Ingrave, St. Nicholas Dated 1735, by an unknown architect, with a very impressive red brick western tower.

Inworth, All Saints South door with head of four-centred arcuation, heavily rear framed, and heavily reinforced with iron work. Its front face is divided into four vertical panels. Nave roof has crown posts and seven cants—all varnished.

Kelvedon, St. Mary the Virgin A fine nave roof, illustrated in Plate VI. This has arch-braced tie beams, the braces being of four-centred curvature; the rafters above the ties are arched to the ridge piece with four timbers and the wall-piece spandrels are traceried. The west frame is arched to the ridge piece, which is diagonally set and has pendants beneath it. At the half-bay intervals there are extended sole pieces with figure carvings above them. The chancel roof is of seven cants, and good.

Kelvedon Hatch, St. Nicholas 1895, by J. T. Newman.

Kirby-le-Soken, St. Michael Restored 1870.

Laindon, St. Nicholas The western timber belfry of this church is its most important feature, and is described on p. 69. The nave roof is in two bays separated by a tie beam on wall pieces with knees. It is probably of the 15th century, and the knees have a four-centred curvature. This beam carries a crown post having a chamfered stem, and left thick at head and foot; the common rafters form seven cants. The south aisle, or chapel, is of the 14th century and has a seven-canted roof that could be of the same age but lacks datable features. The chancel roof is extremely fine, in seven cants and panelled, its main frames being arched to the collars; it has crested wall plates. See Plate X. The south door is good and could date as the doorway, heavily rear framed and strap-hinged. South porch of timber but extensively rebuilt, with two carved knees retained. West of the belfry is the Priest's House, probably of the close of the 16th century or the earliest decades of the 17th century, since it is plank-clad in the New England manner. It has three tie beams, north to south, and heavy cambered collars with side purlins, to which the common rafters are pegged.

Lamarsh, Holy Innocents Some early planks on the south door, and the south porch has a floor beneath the roof. The joists of this floor are fitted by means of barefaced soffit tenons, moulded scotia-cyma, c. 14th century.

Langdon Hills, St. Mary the Virgin and All Saints Nave roof crown post in two bays, plastered over. Chancel in seven cants, with collar purlin and inclined ashlar pieces.

Langenhoe, St. Mary 1886 of old materials.

114

Langford, St. Giles With western apse, but all visible timbers date from the 'restoration' of 1882.

Langham, St. Mary All carpentry appears to be of the 19th century. Entry not gained, but clear glass windows made the foregoing statement possible.

Langley, St. John the Evangelist Nave roof a contradiction, since it is of four bays divided by five tie beams, above which is a double-hammerbeam assembly with, in addition, saltire bracing above the collars. All richly carved with folded leaf, and with wall pieces of Perpendicular section. The date could be either late 15th or early 16th century. There are side purlins at collar height, which may be an addition.

Latchingdon, St. Michael Nave roof in two bays, divided by a tie beam of the section which typifies the years 1475–1500, with seven cants above. There is a western belfry standing on four jowled and massive posts, and lacking arch bracing. South porch with a 17th-century roof having side purlins and collars.

Latton, St. Mary the Virgin South porch a good example of the late 16th or very early 17th century, with trenched collars, and flattened, four-centred heads to the side openings.

Lawford, St. Mary The south porch embodies some 14th-century timbers which are of great interest.

Layer Breton, St. Mary 1923.

Layer de la Haye, St. John the Baptist South porch of timber, with trenched collars and very good verge boards. It has six couples of rafters and the face tie beam is seated in barefaced lap dovetails—possibly of the close of the 14th century. The nave roof is in seven cants and has wall plates that may indicate a late 15th-century date.

Layer Marney, St. Mary the Virgin South porch roofed in five cants, six couples. The south door is Tudor in shape and made of nailed cross boards. The nave roof is of seven cants with four commons per bay, the principal frames are well moulded right round the cants with heavy tie beams. This roof dates from Lord Marney's rebuilding, in 1520–25, as does the chancel, with tolerable certainty. The chancel roof is interesting, in seven cants with inclined ashlars, side purlins (cf. Ingatestone) above the collars and compassed wind-braces that rise to the apexes of the principal rafters. See Fig. 36.

Leaden Roding, St. Michael Nave roof of seven cants with double collars and five closely spaced tie beams, this is framed into seven cants. The inner wall plate is double, has both wave mouldings and beaks, and this fact together with the double collars should indicate a date in the 14th century. The chancel roof is also of seven cants but of less certain date, and has been much rebuilt at the eaves. The western belfry makes no pretensions, and is in all probability Tudor. The turret was not examined.

Leigh, St. Clement Fifteenth-century north aisle with original timber roof.

Lexden, St. Leonard 1820–21.

Leyton, St. Mary the Virgin Not examined, but essentially of 1832.

Lindsell, St. Mary the Virgin According to the local guidebook the tie beams of the nave were added during the 17th century, and the ceiling boards removed in 1938, when the 14th-century roof was restored. The tie beams in question are hollow-chamfered, as are the inner wall plates, which tenon into the beams' flanks with a mason's mitre at the junction. The source of the guidebook's information is not known, but there is no reason why the timbers should not be earlier, or the surmounting roof of seven cants earlier than the same ascription, i.e. 14th century. Certainly these roof timbers have been moved at some time, and subsequently mixed with others that embody different jointing techniques. A roof of considerable interest: an important feature that has survived, at the west gable only, is a pair of rafters with a short king post set on their collar, and braces beneath—reminiscent of the apse roof at East Ham (q.v.). Of equal interest is a surviving sole piece, visible under the northern chancel eaves, and another close to the chancel arch. These are stepped down and the rafters' feet lapped to their sides. The chancel roof is of seven cants, and while its date is uncertain, it would be of the 14th century at the latest.

Liston, Dedication not known Nave roof in seven obtuse cants. These are ceiled and pargetted and show the date 1701, with the initials I.S. The chancel has an excellent roof of six cants which is panelled, has figure carvings on its principals, and a 'honeysuckle' crested wall plate (see plate XXXII). The south door is of interest.

Little Baddow, St. Mary the Virgin Very sadly restored so far as the roofs are concerned. The chancel was evidently of seven cants, and has been re-worked. The nave, which is of unusual width, is covered with a strange roof apparently of contemporary date and most unsatisfactory appearance. One old tie beam at the west end is mounted on knees and wall pieces with stone corbels. The south porch is of interest, and probably late 16th-century in origin; its five couples have trenched collars, and its north tie beam is acutely cranked.

Little Bardfield, St. Katherine Late Saxon west tower, which had its timber floors and parapeted spire rebuilt during the Decorated period (c. 1250–1350). It is evident that much of the timber used at that time was re-used, and it seems logical that it derived from the original build. Many finely cut and unusual timbers, possibly from the bell chamber and its frames, during the Confessor's reign. Nave roof in two bays with a tall crown post, centrally, and short posts set on stone corbels at east and west ends. There are deep wall pieces standing on stone semi-octagonal corbels with plain scroll mouldings which recur on the inner wall plates—the scroll moulding had its maximum popularity between c. 1280 and c. 1340 (H. Forrester, 1972, 31).

Little Bentley, St. Mary the Virgin The nave roof is carried on single hammerbeams and is steeply arched to its collars on which short king posts are mounted to carry the ridge piece, see Plate XXXIII. North aisle Perpendicular, with good roof.

Little Braxted, St. Nicholas Norman nave with apsed chancel of the same period. The apse roof is scissor-braced through the collars (see Fig. 8), and has an apparently unique semi-circular collar that is splay-scarfed in mid curve: probably late 13th century. The scissors recur for a few couples at the west end, but the main length of the nave has an equally remarkable roof which has side purlins with common collars, and steep curved bracing. The north aisle is of 1884, as is the vestry. The belfry has not been examined.

116

Little Bromley, St. Mary the Virgin The nave has some early sole pieces, but no other timber of interest. Good south porch, and interesting doors north and south.

Little Burstead, St. Mary All timber items here are of great interest, and the church begins with a Norman nave. Nave roof in two bays, with quadrate crown post and seven cants, plastered. See Fig. 24. Chancel roof also with a crown post on a tie beam with wall pieces, arch braces and tracery spandrels. Both roofs of the 15th century, at which time the roof of the church was raised — see earlier cap stone in west gable. The belfry is a small one, as is proportionate to the church, but is quite elaborate and most interesting: this is described on p. 67, and shown in Plate XXIII. The south door is good and would date either as the doorway — which it fits well enough — or as the extensive rebuilding of somewhere between 1425 and 1500. It is strap-hinged and clad with hump-faced and rebated planks.

Littlebury, Holy Trinity Much restored in 1870-75 by E. Barr. Roofs quite ambitious, of softwood. One door, the north, is cross-planked.

Little Chesterford, St. Mary the Virgin Has a long nave and chancel under one roof, and the general fabric appears to be of the 13th century. The roof is of seven bays and features Perpendicular mouldings that may date from the 16th century. Each tie beam carries principal rafters that are collared, by tenons, and fitted with one butt purlin per slope. There are eight common rafters per bay, with ashlar pieces. The porch has extremely interesting wall plates.

Little Clacton, St. James Nave and chancel both roofed in seven cants, the nave having been much altered and impaired. Information displayed within the church, which is attributed to Mr. Gurney Benham, but not dated, states that the nave was lengthened in 1346, the bell turret built in 1415, and the porch added in 1381. The ascription of the porch is extremely probable and in view of the exactitude of the date it is equally probable that a document indicates its building date. This porch has a crown-post roof, lacks side tracery, and employs numerous heavy hanging knees. The verge boards are cusped in the same manner as at White Notley, and the entrance is formed by two massive durns. The belfry is shown in Fig. 61, and described on p. 69.

Little Coggeshall, St. Nicholas The *capella-extra-muros* of the former Cistercian Abbey. A wealth of information about this building is displayed in the west end, and from this, as from other sources, it appears that the chapel was built during the time of Abbot Benedict, 1218-23. The roof is composed of 25 couples of common rafters with tenoned collars and trenched scissor braces — the latter are fitted with secret notched laps at their feet. The precise decade during which the 'open' form of the notched lap joint was superseded by the 'secret' form has been discovered. This change evidently occurred during the 'break' in the building of Wells Cathedral, Somerset — between 1209 and *c.* 1213. This was during the time of Bishop Jocelyn, from 1206 to 1242. It is a fact which confirms the looser dating of this event which could previously be deduced only from this *capella-extra-muros*; it may well indicate earlier ascriptions for other examples of such joints in church timberwork.

A part of the original wall plate has also survived. The roof is shown in Fig. 7, and described on p. 9.

Little Dunmow, St. Mary The roof is very high, and has tie beams and seven cants above them. It may incorporate some early components.

Little Hallingbury, St. Mary the Virgin Has a chancel roof of great interest (see Plate XI), which is of single hammerbeam category with richly roll-moulded component timbers and leaf-carved wall plates—the whole being late Perpendicular. Escutcheons are affixed to the hammers' ends, of very curly shape. The common couples have cambered collars, to which arch braces rise from their ashlar pieces. The south door has a good rear frame with oblique ledges, fitted with barefaced dovetails, while the front is in four panels with cinquefoiled heads. South porch good, of timber, with unusual side traceries—14th century.

Little Horkesley, St. Peter and St. Paul Destroyed by a bomb, 1940.

Little Laver, St. Mary the Virgin Nave roof in three bays of five common couples, with three tie beams of flat section having no wall pieces. Above, the roof is of seven cants, with double collars, of the 14th century.

Little Leighs, St. John the Evangelist An early nave and chancel, the first roofed in seven cants above straight tie beams, and the chancel of seven cants which are ceiled. At the outer edge the nave sole pieces are laid on individual, thin, wooden plates. At the western end is a small bell turret and spire, mounted on one tie beam and two wall pieces (see Fig. 59). This is mentioned on p. 69.

Little Maplestead, St. John the Baptist The bell turret and spire are of late 19th-century soft wood, as is also the roof of the nave. The apsidal chancel may be of interest, since it has an apsidal roof, in four cants, causing the convergence of no less than 16 collars. All this is heavily painted, or stencilled, and may relate to the restoration.

Little Oakley, St. Mary Locked and key unobtainable.

Little Saling *see* **Bardfield Saling, St. Peter and St. Paul**

Little Sampford, St. Mary the Virgin North porch with roof in three cants, boarded on underside. South porch of *c.* 1700, with trenched collar roof of five couples. Nave and chancel roofs both flattish, camberbeam, and Perpendicular.

Little Tey, St. James the Less Nave and chancel in one and with apsidal east end, over which the roof has a square gable—on plan. Both roofs are of seven cants, without any tie beams, and with ancient framing at the eaves triangles. The belfry is a later addition, demonstrable by the fact of the west light having its head removed to make way for a flat cill to carry the two western corner posts. The turret is saltire-braced, without lap jointing, but nevertheless of great age. It is carried by a transom beam protruding right through the nave wall, which is supported on posts that have been hidden by thin casing —as have the two braces. The north doorway contains an oaken frame, the lintel of which supports the masonry tympanum (Norman) and is fitted with a big oak socket at its centre, for the top of a vertical locking bar of timber. This frame is rebated all round, to receive a square door.

Little Totham, All Saints Substantial evidence of the Norman beginnings, but no timber of the same period. The chancel is roofed in seven cants and has an inner wall plate that could reproduce an earlier one. The nave is crossed by three tie beams, of which the western one may well have supported a belfry in the past; while the eastern one has mouldings of 14th-century character with wall pieces set on well carved human head corbels—solid knees fill the angles. Not only do the eastern and central beams and wall pieces differ in section, and age, but their respective wall plates show the same dissimilarity. The central beam is some time during the Perpendicular period. The west tower base is of squared flints and is dated 1527 on an escutcheon, carved over the four-centred west doorway. Above this is an interesting timber tower—see Fig. 63, and p. 72—incorporating one re-used 14th-century floor.

Little Wakering, St. Mary the Virgin Nave roof of two bays with two cambered tie beams, crown posts, and five couples per bay of rafters framed in seven cants. The crown posts are octagonal in section and have capital and base treatment of early character, roll-moulded. Tower of 1412 surmounted by a needle spire, not examined.

Little Waltham, St. Martin Nave roof with scissor braces through its collars—a good copy apparently, and dated 1883. The chancel roof is arched to its collars, also of 1883. The only rewarding piece of carpentry is the south door with V-edged boards and simply framed, possibly early 16th century.

Little Warley, St. Peter South door planked with V-edged boards having scotia-moulded overlaps, and strap hinges, of uncertain date. The nave has a chamfered central tie beam with a thick, quadrate crown post and seven cants.

Little Wigborough, St. Nicholas The general fabric seems to be of the late 15th century, and was heavily restored after the earthquake of 1884. The existing nave roof seems to be of the 16th century, has two purlins in each slope, collars that are tenoned, and wall pieces with braces and ashlar-pieces.

Little Yeldham, St. John the Baptist Western belfry on two portal frames aligned north–south, with arch braces of distinctly Tudor arcuation. Turret not ascended. The nave roof can only be examined from under its eaves, where at the south-east it can be seen that its ashlar, sole and rafter triangle is framed in the manner originating at the end of the 13th century.

Loughton, St. John the Baptist 1846, by Smirke.

Magdalen Laver, St. Mary Magdalen Nave roof of seven cants with double collars, in two bays with ten common couples per bay. The west tie beam is on wall pieces with arch braces, and carries the two eastern posts of the bell turret. See Fig. 58. It appears that both roof and belfry are of the same build. The chancel is also roofed in seven cants with double collars, in three bays defined by two tie beams—two of which formerly had wall pieces, as is shown by the now empty mortises in their soffits. There is also some very good work in the form of furnishings.

Maldon, All Saints South door good, with humped planks and scotia-moulded face fillets, cross planked and rivetted. The south aisle appears to be *c.* 1340, having Purbeck shafts to its arcade. The roof to it is in seven cants, plastered, and the tie beams are richly moulded and steeply humped. The ancient tower with spire and three spirelets not ascended.

St. Mary the Virgin The tower, the upper part of which dates to 1636, contains all the carpentry of this church. The stairs and spire are of great interest, and date from the time of the tower repairs.

Manningtree, St. Michael and all Angels Demolished.

Manuden, St. Mary Nave roof with octagonal crown posts having 'crenellated' capitals and bell-spread feet, of the Perpendicular style, each with four braces—the whole upon moulded wall plates. Roof to north transept apparently of the late Decorated, also with octagonal crown posts, having four braces each, of square section and steep pitches.

Margaret Roding, St. Margaret Nave roof in seven cants, apparently of the 19th century, but supported by two medieval crown posts and tie beams. The chancel has a central tie beam of hollow-moulded 14th-century section. The wall plates are also of late 14th-century type, but the existing roof is also of 19th-century scissor braces. In the chancel is an extremely interesting carved timber, floral corbel.

Margaretting, St. Margaret A church that is uncommonly rich in medieval carpenters' works, all of which have survived in good order. Taken in order of magnitude the belfry must, of course, come first. This is based on an east–west colonnade of massive posts (see description on p. 76). Secondly, the roof of the nave, which is an important example, arched to its collars, which are surmounted by crown pieces and collar purlin (illustrated in Fig. 28, and described on p. 29). The chancel has two bays of panelled and seven-canted roofing. The south aisle has a narrow roof also of seven cants. The door in the north wall of the nave is of the early Perpendicular, of eight V-edged planks, strap-hinged and well framed at its rear, with square lap jointing. The timber porch, extending to the north, which is illustrated in Plate XX and discussed on pp. 56 and 58, is a very good specimen of the 15th century.

Marks Tey, St. Andrew Nave roof of seven cants, chancel roof also of seven cants, and with an interesting wall plate, possibly of the 14th century. It can be seen at the eaves that the sole pieces tenon into the rafters' feet. The west tower suffered damage during the siege of Colchester in 1648 (L.G.B.) and had its upper part replaced with a timber tower of slightly later date. This is shown in Fig. 64, and further described on p. 72, and is vertically clad with boards. The south porch is a very interesting one, of rather late date, which is illustrated in Fig. 52, and further discussed on p. 61.

Mashbury, Dedication not known Nave roof, apparently 19th century, in seven cants; chancel roof arched to the collars. In the west bay are traces of a small timber belfry, with two reinforcing posts that appear to be of the 17th century. In the south doorway, which is Norman, is a plain rectangular door in three planks with a light rear frame, of Perpendicular period.

120

Matching, St. Mary the Virgin Both nave and chancel roofs are apparently the work of Sir A. Blomfield in 1875. The nave roof is arched to the collars with crown posts above, and both north and south aisles, like the chancel, also have Victorian roofs. The south porch may incorporate some later medieval timbers.

Mayland, St. Barnabas By the younger Hardwick, 1867.

Messing, All Saints Extremely good nave roof (see Fig. 16, and p. 17), totalling five bays, two of which at the west end are largely of the 1840 restoration. It is datable to *c.* 1360 by the heraldic achievement carved on one of the principal ashlar pieces, at the foot. These would pertain to Thomas Baynard who would have held the manor of Messing at that time—the achievement bears his label of five, indicating that he was the eldest son of Thomas Baynard the first, d. 1344. The roof has a good single hammerbeam frame designed to clear the chancel arch, and thereafter it is arched to the collars, in an ingenious and economical manner. The common rafters are framed into seven cants.

Middleton, All Saints There is a very great deal of good carpenters' work in this church. The nave roof is in three bays and had an integral belfry, framed on the westernmost tie beam. The free transverse frame at the centre of the roof has its tie beam set at the tops of the principal wall pieces, with traceried knees in the angles. There are side purlins, one to each slope, and collars set rather high and carrying short king pieces that support a ridge piece. This roof is illustrated in Fig. 26. The chancel roof is also arched to the collars and ceiled into five cants; the numerous side purlins form square panels that are cusped, in timber. The south door, which is hung in a Norman doorway, is very difficult to date, and is not original.

Mistley, St. Mary Only a flushwork porch survived in 1953.

Moreton, St. Mary the Virgin Nave roof of seven cants, ceiled with plaster; two very tall crown posts have survived the restoration of 1868-9, and are at the west end of the nave. These two posts are laterally braced, down to their tie beams, indicating an early origin.

Mount Bures, St. John No timber work visible.

Mountnessing, St. Giles The western timber belfry here is very good, and in some respects unusual among its kind, having cruck-type shores to north and south. The nave roof is crown post and seven cants, built in two bays. The crown posts are very tall, of octagonal section, and fitted with four braces of peculiarly small size and curvature.

Mucking, St. John the Baptist 1849-52, except for many parts of the masonry. Locked and not examined.

Mundon, St. Mary Now in the care of The Friends of Friendless Churches, which Trust has had some restoration works effected on the western timber tower. The north porch is the finest example of its kind seen in the county. It is illustrated in Fig. 53, under the section on Porches, in which it is fully described. The nave is roofed in three bays, with two tie beams carrying crown posts of clearly different ages. Those at the western end both have two braces only, to the collar purlin, and the eastern example is earlier and has four braces. The belfry is small and good, and has lacked its surmounting spire for many years.

Navestock, St. Thomas the Apostle This church was very extensively shaken by a land mine during World War II. The most important feature is, of course, the belfry which has been carbon-dated to 1193. This is fully described in the sections on Belfries, at p. 62. The door leading into the belfry is of interest, and must date with the south aisle c. 1255. The south arcade has piers of timber, which were faked, with small timbers and much plaster, to look like stone. The arches were also of timber, faced as stone (Hewett and Smith, 1972). The chancel is of the 14th century and retains, on view, its central and original tie beam with traceried knees beneath each end. Both the chancel south door and the nave door are of interest in view of the iron work they carry.

Nazeing, All Saints South porch of timber studwork with closed-in sides, ridged roof with pierced and cusped verge boards. Inside a two-bay roof of obtuse pitch with roll-moulded tie beams of the thin soffited type exploited by Cardinal Morton at Lambeth Palace, in 1490 (Hewett, 1980, 210). Three rafters in each bay, moulded wall plate. Interesting door leaf, probably contemporary with the porch. Nave roof in eight bays with the principals arched to their collars, having roll-moulded arrises—Perpendicular, as is the north arcade. Chancel with a two-bay crown-post roof, the posts of cross-quadrate section with four braces, hollow-moulded wall plates. North aisle with an unusual roof: crown-posted with four bays, the tie beams always sloped down to meet the north wall—the crown posts vertical with two braces. All moulded, seven couples per bay. Both nave and aisle roofs probably date, as do the arcade piers to the mid-15th century.

Nevendon, St. Peter Nave roof in two bays with seven-canted frames, straight tie beams and crown posts stop-chamfered in such a manner as to create an impression of a capital and a base. The little bell turret is mounted on a pair of western tie beams, its vertical members carrying the bell frame directly. Of uncertain date. The chancel is also crown post, in two bays.

Newport, St. Mary the Virgin The nave clerestory is 15th-century and is roofed with a rather new-looking queen post assembly. It has one side purlin in each slope, and some angel corbels, in timber, at the half bays.

Noak Hill, St. Thomas By Blore, 1841–42.

North Benfleet, All Saints Only a belfry of heavy timbers is visible in the western bay of the nave. It is of portal frames having arch braces of Tudor curvature. Its former turret exists, as high as to the rafters, and is braced in 15th-century fashion. The ceiled nave roof is in seven cants.

North End, Black Chapel May have been built by Augustinian canons during the 15th century, and is hence upon unconsecrated ground. The oaken structure of the nave is good, with knees under tie beams and wall plates, with plastered roof of seven cants. The chancel has a spur-tied end frame, to take the east window.

North Fambridge, Holy Trinity 18th-century brick.

122

North Shoebury, St. Mary the Virgin Nave roof with octagonal crown posts having slender shafts, and four braces of a thickness equal to the posts, finished in seven cants. Early Perpendicular. The wall plates are deeply hollow-moulded, yet have crenellations along their tops. The tie beams have wall pieces with traceried spandrels in their braces.

North Weald Bassett, St. Andrew Contemporary, due to recent fire.

Norton Mandeville, All Saints Heavily restored, with some early crown posts surviving in the nave.

Orsett, St. Giles and All Saints A church almost destroyed by fire in 1926, and it is difficult to determine the past vicissitudes of the roofs as a result of the rebuilding. The south porch has a crown-post roof, three couples either side of the central tie beam, of Perpendicular section. The nave roof is continuous with that of the chancel, and is essentially Perpendicular in character and mouldings. It is constructed in five bays, the central ones having crown posts with four braces, collar purlin, and seven cants. The tie beams are set on wall pieces with arch braces having four pierced, cusped lancets in their spandrels. The west end has a frame that is arched to the collar, and mounts a short crown post to receive the end of the collar purlin; there are also trenched scissor braces throughout. All principal frames are good quality carpentry, and undoubtedly Perpendicular, but above the collars everything may date from after the fire.

Ovington, St. Mary The roof at present is ceiled with plaster, apparently at collar height, producing five cants. There are six bays and seven frames, with an unusual longitudinal timber running at the height of the joint between the ashlar pieces and the rafters. The purpose of this cannot be seen owing to the plastering. The late 16th or early 17th century is the probable period of this work. There is a small belfry at the west end, on two portal frames, braced heavily, from north to south only.

Panfield, St. Mary The nave roof is an interesting example of crown post, collar purlin and seven cants, having inclined ashlar pieces. The central crown post is quadrate in section and stands on a moderately cambered tie beam, implying the 15th century. There are deep wall pieces and solid hanging knees beneath, of Tudor arcuation. The eastern end has a curious frame of two timbers that are cranked to the collar, having a short crown piece above the collar to support the end of the purlin. See Fig. 31. The western end of the collar purlin is convincingly framed into the timber belfry that occupies the west bay of the nave, with two portal frames, north-south, and arch braces of early Perpendicular curvature. The best carpentry, however, is the south porch, a wholly timber example that is illustrated in Fig. 44.

Pattiswick, St. Mary Both nave and chancel roofs of great interest, the nave roof being illustrated in Figs. 14 and 15. The nave has a central tie beam with straight soffit and subtly cambered top surface, which is reduced in width by chamfers each side. On this is the crown post, octagonal in section, and having a carved capital formed by three scroll mouldings of increased diameters. This must indicate a date during the period 1260–1340, during the transition from Decorated to Perpendicular styles. This roof is separated from that of the chancel by a timber-framed gable.

123

The roof of the chancel is 'trussed' in seven cants, and has an unusual inner 'wall plate' mounted in front of the sole pieces' ends. The section of this suggests the 15th century, but the roof itself is earlier. The west bell turret is carried on two straight tie beams, and retains timbers of interest inside; its exterior was recently thoroughly renovated. There is a south porch with a good roof; side purlin and with ogee wind braces in the pitch plane, c. 1490.

Pebmarsh, St. John the Baptist Nave roof with queen posts on straight tie beams, and one purlin in each slope. The tie beams are straight and without wall pieces, whilst the queen posts have curved wind braces to the purlins, which are set 'in-pitch'. The wall plates are cavetto moulded, and the date most uncertain. In both north and south aisles stone plate hooks may be seen, which would have carried the headers of the lean-to roofs at the time of first building.

Peldon, St. Mary the Virgin Nave roof is a very good hammerbeam example, datable as the clerestory to the early 16th century.

Pentlow, St. George Contains no carpentry of interest.

Pitsea, St. Michael 1871, by Sir A. Blomfield.

Plaistow Three churches of the 19th century.

Pleshey, Holy Trinity 1868 by Chancellor.

Prittlewell, Annunciation of the Blessed Virgin South door of the early 16th century with panels of crocketted ogee arches, and a chancel roof richly coloured and gilt, with angel hammerbeams.

Purleigh, All Saints Nave roof of pitchpine, hammerbeamed, with scissor braces and collar purlin. This roof is attributable to Dr. Hatch in 1880. The chancel and aisle roofs are of equally little merit. The north door has V-edged planks and strap hinges and is medieval. The south porch is of brick with a good roof having terminal crown posts and roll-moulded plates. The south door has a very good outer face with much unusual iron work on a Victorian rear frame.

Quendon, of unknown dedication Restored in 1881, to which date may be ascribed the roof of the nave, magnificently coloured and gilt with side purlins.

Radwinter, St. Mary the Virgin The south porch is unique in Essex in that it is dragonbeamed, and probably of 1250–1350. This is shown in Fig. 42, and described on p. 51. Despite the fact that the church was rebuilt by Eden Nesfield in 1869–70, it retains a nave roof of the 14th century. This is built in four bays, has five tie beams with wall pieces and traceried spandrel knees of good quality. The crown posts have doubly jowled heads and receive the collar purlin in a trench between the jowls. The tie beams are straight. The north door is of interest, with a Decorated arcature, a rear frame of six stiles and eight ledges rivetted through roves, and hollow moulded face members.

Rainham, St. Helen and St. Giles Chancel roof in seven cants with crown post of quadrate cross section. The rafters are moulded, apparently a mixture of early and 19th-century components. The nave roof is a Victorian reproduction of what, presumably, existed before restoration. It is also crown post with seven cants. The north door is Norman and built of vertical and diagonal planks; the vertical face planks are rebated, and there is a portion of one of the strap hinges.

Ramsden Bellhouse, St. Mary Extensively rebuilt in 1880, but retaining the west belfry, which is one of the larger and more impressive examples. The nave roof also pre-dates the rebuilding and is in three bays with crown posts, collar purlin and seven cants. One western tie beam was formerly wall pieced, as the plugged soffit mortises indicate, and the eastern tie beam carries an elaborate Tudor crown post. All the sole pieces in the nave are carved at their projecting inner ends. The chancel roof is in two bays, with a central crown post having a Tudor arcuation to its two purlin braces.

Ramsden Crays, St. Mary 1871; not examined.

Ramsey, St. Michael The nave roof is of 14th-century style, with crown posts and seven cants, much repaired. The chancel has an excellent roof dated 1597. See Plate XVIII, and description on p. 41. The south door is, or rather once was, an excellent specimen, the outer face of which has been severely defaced—probably at the Reformation.

Rawreth, St. Nicholas All carpentry of interest is confined to the west tower, the belfry floor, frames and roof.

Rayleigh, Holy Trinity The first floor in the west tower dates from 1396 according to a document in the church which specifies the date of building of the tower itself. The nave roof is of five and a half bays with five tie beams, the ties are straight and the bays short with five common rafters per bay. The north chapel, of St. John the Baptist, has a good roof in seven cants, probably dating from the late 15th century.

Rayne, All Saints 1840, with a late Tudor west tower in red brick.

Rettendon, All Saints The nave roof is in oak, of the last century apparently. The roof over the north aisle is, in contrast, most rewarding. This roof is arched to the collars, with two massive arch timbers reaching far down the wall pieces; the common couples are framed into seven cants, and have *compassed ashlar pieces, and compassed soulaces*—this places them in the category of those at Danbury, dating them either to c. 1300, or to the very beginning of the Perpendicular. There are twin wall plates, without recourse to sole pieces. There are seven couples per bay.

Rickling, All Saints Nave roof in seven cants, Victorian, and executed in resinous soft wood. It has an inner wall plate similar to the one in Coggeshall Abbey. The chancel roof is also Victorian.

Ridgewell, St. Laurence The south porch has a good camberbeam roof in two bays, and with wall pieces; the mouldings of both plates and 'joists' indicate a date of c. 1450. The nave roof is extremely fine, arched to the collars, and having very short hammerbeams on alternate frames. This roof is shown in Plate IV, and described on p. 31. The chancel roof is scissor braced, the braces tenoned at their lower ends, and the wall plates are crenellated.

Rivenhall, St. Mary and All Saints 1838–9, brick.

Romford, St. Edward the Confessor 1849–50 by T. Johnson.

Roxwell, St. Michael and All Angels Nave roof of seven cants with three tie beams and tall ashlar pieces, its date uncertain. One post, at least, of the western belfry is ancient, although the structure is attributed to 1891. The chancel is really rewarding with scissor braces having tenoned end joints, of the 13th century. There is one tie beam near the centre and the sole pieces are dove-tailed into the tops of the inner wall plates. The period 1270–1300 is proposed for this roof.

Roydon, St. Peter The nave appears to be of the 13th century, and the north aisle is of *c.* 1330; but while the north aisle roof endorses the date ascription for that part of the building, the roof of the nave should, by all known criteria, be a good deal earlier than any masonry features suggest. The latter is illustrated in Figure 4 and discussed on page 4. The nave roof, so far as the present index is concerned, is of seven cants, and unusually framed—mainly with open notched laps. Above the collars there are two V-struts, also notch-lapped into position. The ashlar pieces have notch-lapped upper ends, comparable to those found by H. Deneux to date between *c.* 1040 and *c.* 1260. It is built in four bays, the most westerly of which has been replaced by the architects recently engaged in repairing the church after damage by fire.

The north aisle roof is a good crown-post example which must logically date from the first completion of that aisle, *c.* 1330, It is finished in seven cants; the eastern bay is also coved, with compassed timbers placed under the collar purlin. There is also a fine and interesting screen. The tower was not examined.

Runwell, St. Mary Possessing two very good timber porches, both crown post with traceried side lights, that on the north being illustrated in Fig. 49 on p. 57.

Saffron Walden, St. Mary the Virgin Almost 200 feet long and lavishly roofed in richly carved timber, this has become an essentially Perpendicular building owing to a massive rebuilding which took place between *c.* 1450 and *c.* 1525. The nave roof, built in seven bays, is camberbeam with wall pieces that have traceried spandrels to their arch braces, which are of four-centred curvature. There is also a four-centred arcading in timber between each successive pair of camberbeams. The mouldings are rich assortments of Perpendicular rolls, and perhaps the last decade of the rebuilding period would be the most appropriate for this roof, illustrated in Plate XII. The chancel has a roof of six bays with deep wall pieces, carved with standing figures at their bases, which has been ascribed to the close of the 15th century and which is illustrated in Plate XIII.

The south aisle roof is low-pitched above straight-soffitted tie beams, having wall pieces resting on the masonry columns attached to the walls and very simply traceried in the spandrels of their four-centred arch braces. Above the ties are four small, and one principal, struts; a roof similar to that at Newport. The north aisle roof is almost identical, and probably of the same date.

St. Osyth, St. Peter and St. Paul The south porch, of 16th-century red brick, has a roof that is apparently contemporary, comprising six couples with very high, trenched collars and a tie beam each end. The nave roof is a very elegant single hammerbeam, framed with slender component timbers, and a ridge piece and three purlins in each slope. The wall pieces carrying the hammerbeams have double-ogee mouldings and indicate a date in the period 1450–1500, if considered with the double rolls planed onto both purlins and wall plates. The chancel has a roof in three cants apparently of very late date. The north aisle has a five-bay canted-beam roof with folded leaf carved along its principals, pendants and wall pieces with knees; the south aisle a canted-beam roof of *c.* 1500–25 with roll-moulded principal members and wall pieces. The transepts have small roofs that resemble floors in view of their small area and flatness.

Salcott, St. Mary An interesting south door, or pair of doors, with central shuts, illustrated in Fig. 84. The front is treated in the linenfold manner, but the ends severely simplified and dating apparently from the early decades of the 15th century. The rear frame is well jointed at every point, and uses only barefaced lap dovetails. The remainder of the work must date from 1884, when the church was repaired after the earthquake.

Sandon, St. Andrew The nave has substantial fragments of one single hammerbeam frame, in which the outer ends of the hammers clasp the principal rafters in the same manner as do the collars at the nave of St. Katherine's church, Gosfield—probably therefore *c.* 1430. The hammerposts are tenoned into the rafters, and have traceried knees with quatrefoil reliefs in each face. The chancel has a roof of seven cants, ceiled with planks, and dated by an agreement with a mason to pull down and rebuild the said chancel, of 1348. (St. Paul's MS no. 1264.) Although no timber roof appears to be specified it is a reasonable assumption that the existing one would date from the termination of the mason's contract. The wall plates (interior) now to be seen at Sandon have a double-roll moulding on their chamfers, and while this is considered to be a Perpendicular feature it must be remembered that it also occurred at Coggeshall Abbey in *c.* 1220.

Shalford, St. Andrew South door early Perpendicular with good 14th-century tracery, see Fig. 83. The roofs, other than that of the chancel, are also early Perpendicular and the chancel itself has a simple roof of seven cants, probably of the early 14th century.

Sheering, St. Mary the Virgin The nave has a rare and very interesting roof, which is of the Decorated style and 14th century. This roof is built in three frames with tie beams set on wall pieces with arch braces. Above these ties the roof is literally a gambrel one, with two pitches meeting at the single side purlins which are on top of the queen posts, and in the centre there is a king post carrying a ridge piece. Both queen and king posts are fitted with numerous knees at their upper ends, and the two bays have 15 common rafters each. (Plate XXXIV.)

The chancel, which is roofed in two bays, has a side purlin each slope and these are housed in the collars, from which arch braces run down the principal rafters to the tops of their ashlar pieces. The side purlins are wind braced, the braces being of flattened, four-centred arcuation, 16th century. The south door is good, of the late 14th century; the face of it bears vertical mouldings and one moulded rail across the centre, while its rear frame has four stiles under ledges with full lap-dovetail ends, and two—top and bottom —with barefaced lap dovetails.

Shelley, St. Peter 1888, by Habershon & Fawckner.

Shellow Bowells, St. Peter and St. Paul 1754, but not examined.

Shenfield, St. Mary the Virgin South porch with three crown posts of quadrate section and six cinquefoil lights each side, probably of the late 15th century. The chancel has a seven canted roof that cannot be examined closely, while the nave has one quadrate sectioned crown post which has been retained at the west end, standing on a heavy and cambered tie beam and evidently part of a former seven canted roof. The rest is now ceiled over. The north arcade is of timber, and has seven oaken piers, each having four round shafts with four hollows between them—Perpendicular. The timber belfry is one of the major examples of its kind in this county, with an impressively tall and slender spire, the top 25 feet of which was skilfully rebuilt in this century.

Shopland, St. Mary Demolished 1957-8.

Sible Hedingham, St. Peter South porch with camber-beam roof having double-ogee mouldings on its main timbers, indicative of a date between *c.* 1370 and *c.* 1550. It is in two bays each with four common rafters. Good, carved bosses. A magnificent roof exists in the two western bays of the south aisle, which has pendants, a ridge piece (at the top of the camber) and cable ornament together with spiral foliage.

South Benfleet, St. Mary The nave has been re-roofed, doubtless several times, but when this was last done in 1902 some very interesting flat, straight tie beams were retained—the date of which would be of great interest could it be determined. The chancel roof seems relatively undisturbed and has three crown posts, octagonal with Perpendicular caps and bases, surmounted by seven cants that have been plastered. The tie beams are of remarkable section. The glory of this church is its south porch, with single hammerbeam roof, unusually fine quality side traceries, and verge boards of the 15th century. This is described under the heading of Porches and their development, and illustrated in Fig. 45.

Southchurch, Holy Trinity The local guide here publishes an engraving of the church made from a drawing of 1830, which shows a Norman nave with bell turret and tall brooch spire, and an early Decorated chancel. However, in 1906 and again in 1932, huge additions were built that dwarf this old church, and reduce it to a south aisle. In the west end of the former nave stands a timber belfry, which was of two portal frames aligned north–south and much reinforced in the 17th century, as witness the inscription cut into the additional posts—'I.A. 1666'. The extra posts were, as was usual, inserted under the central part of the north–south transoms. The turret and spire were not ascended. The nave roof is ceiled, but of seven cants, as is also the chancel, and either of these, if inspected, could prove to be of great age.

South Fambridge, All Saints 1846.

South Hanningfield, St. Peter West belfry on two portal frames, restored out of existence; the framing in the north and south sides is still of interest, and probably 14th century. The nave roof has tie beams set on wall pieces with arch braces, and is finished in seven cants. Its date is uncertain.

Southminster, St. Leonard One door in north wall of interest, with V-edged planks having roll-moulded fronts, and strap hinges.

South Ockendon, St. Nicholas Heavily restored and locked. Not examined.

South Shoebury, St. Andrew Nave roof a very interesting example of crown posts (octagonal and with Perpendicular bell-spread feet) and seven cants with inclined ashlar pieces; the tie beams are cambered and set onto wall pieces with solid knees. These are pierced with tracery datable to 1325–50. The wall plates visible inside have long crenellations on their upper edges, and are moulded with shallow hollows of various widths.

South Weald, St. Peter The roof in the new church of 1868, by Teulon, is a magnificent softwood creation, arched to its collars, and much traceried.

Springfield, All Saints Drastically restored, only a small, and late, medieval door remains, in the north of the chancel.

Stambourne, St. Peter and St. Thomas Nave roof in seven cants with roll-moulded tie beams set on wall pieces with arch braces. The cants are plastered over. In the 11th-century west tower there is an interesting roll-moulded joist which is a later insertion. The north aisle roof is of the period 1500–25, having rafters with five roll mouldings in inverted pyramid form. The chancel roof is arched to its collars, with wall pieces datable between *c.* 1525 and *c.* 1550. Each of the arch braces is carved with the motto 'Espoir me Confort'. The underside of this roof is plastered and one can only suspect, or deduce, its excellence.

Stanford-le-Hope, St. Margaret of Antioch Has one roof in seven cants, panelled, and not datable. South door with V-edged planks and ledged at rear.

Stanford Rivers, St. Margaret A very good nave roof in three bays, with quadrate crown posts, collar purlin, and seven cants. The tie beams are on wall pieces with arch braces beneath, having void spandrels. The inner wall plates are of the 15th century, and the wall pieces rest upon scroll-moulded stone corbels. The chancel roof is a very fine example, arched to its collars in single centred arches. These arches are composite, and have ogee and scotia sections, and there are four arch frames. The west bay of the nave is filled with the timber belfry, one of the more impressive examples, standing upon two portal frames aligned north to south, and with elaborate intersecting arch bracing in the side panels at north and south; somewhere in the 14th century. This is illustrated in Fig. 60.

The spire and turret severely damaged by fire, at the time of a recent re-painting, and re-built.

Stansted Moutfitchett Nave, north aisle and chancel, all with carpenters' works apparently dating from the 1888 restoration.

Stanway, St. Albright The nave roof is of interest, being one of the surviving examples that are—or were—scissor-braced. The whole was 'restored' by Sir G. Gilbert Scott in 1880, but at the time of writing eight of the western couples are probably as old as the nave itself. The rafters, and scissors, are squared from very thin and slightly wavy timber, evidently of very few years growth; a couple of rafters now immediately west of the eight scissored couples are heavier in section, and appear to have been principals formerly. They display notched-lap matrices and squint trenches for collars. The north porch is of interest, with crown-post roof and a central tie beam with double hollow chamfers, or mouldings. The roof is of 10 couples.

Stapleford Abbots, St. Mary 1862, by T. Jekyll.

Stapleford Tawney, St. Mary South porch, with quadrate crown post in its roof, six couples, upon stone walls. The nave roof is in seven cants, to which an obscuring, and 19th-century, ceiling has been applied. The chancel roof is also in seven cants, but plastered over. Good, simple, two portal-frame belfry not ascended.

Stebbing, St. Mary the Virgin Generally alleged to be an entirely 14th-century church.The nave roof is flat pitched and not much repaired. The chancel is the roof to view. This must date later than the east window which it almost obstructs; it is a form that is arched to its collars, with diagonal struts, supposed to be in compression, and tracery planks fitted between the braces and the principal rafters, of Decorated character. This roof is properly illustrated and described in the section on Roofing, and is formed in six cants. (See Plate V, and p. 32.)

Steeple, St. Laurence 1844 by F. Chancellor.

Steeple Bumpstead, St. Mary Nave and chancel roofs both Perpendicular with short king posts on tie beams with shallow knees; interesting, and with the chancel roof undergoing repair at the time of examination. The richest piece of carpentry is the roof of the south aisle. The south door is a good one, of Decorated arcuation and built with V-edged planks, strap hinges, and a rear frame comprising two durns, five stiles and 10 ledges which are halved *behind* the stiles. Pegged at curves, and rivetted at its crossings.

Stifford, St. Mary The west tower with its contemporary stair, floors, and surmounting spire—all of the 13th century—is of the greatest interest here. The spire is shown in Fig. 56. The nave roof is of two bays and has a crown post, centrally, upon an almost straight tie beam without wall pieces. The other roofs, among which the chancel and the south aisle are scissored without collars, may date from Palin's 19th-century improvements. The north door is of great interest and loaded with iron of either 12th or 13th centuries, but it is clad with eight V-edged planks which are unlikely to be contemporary. The rear frame is also out of keeping and is built with eight ledges tenoned, or halved, under two straight stiles—one on either side. The curved Romanesque top arch is left unsupported.

Stisted, All Saints This church has suffered massive rebuilding, possibly at the same time (1844) as the tower was built. Little timber has survived, but associated with the former timber of the aisle roofs are the stone plate hooks, provided for the headers of the once lean-to aisle roofs. These must date as the arcades, north *c.* 1180–90, while the south may be later.

Stock Harvard, All Saints The finest carpentered part of this church is, of course, the timber belfry, framed on four vertical posts, and with five three-light west traceries above its door of timber. The nave was severely damaged during World War II and, like the chancel roof which was painted recently, cannot be examined. The north aisle has an interesting crown-post roof, built in three bays; the crown posts are of cross-quadrate section and are carved into various Perpendicular profiles down each arm of the cross, *c.* 1400. The wall-plate profile, and its crenellated upper edge, are also distinctly Perpendicular. The south porch is an interesting one, built in two bays with a crown-post roof and its various arch braces curved in the Decorated style. So it is basically transitional, Decorated–Perpendicular and precise date uncertain. The tie beam is a transom, since it has no dovetailed end joints.

Stondon Massey, St. Peter and St. Paul Nave roof crown post and seven plaster-covered cants. The crown post is of cross-quadrate section, and its four braces have single-centred curvature. Early, but not datable. Belfry in west bay not fully examined.

Stow Maries, St. Mary and St. Margaret The nave was heightened in brick, probably during the 16th century, and now carries a roof that is panelled into a four-centred arch. None of its construction is visible. The chancel has a roof of seven cants, plastered, and unexaminable.

Stratford Three churches, none of which is medieval.

Strethall, St. Mary Chancel roof in seven cants, with crenellated inner wall plates, of uncertain date. The nave roof is in two bays, each of seven common rafters, cambered tie beams on wall pieces with arch braces, Perpendicular. The roof above is also in seven cants. At the tops of the ashlar pieces a curious timber is fitted which resembles a side-purlin; beneath this are numerous ashlar pieces, of which none meets the rafters. It can be seen, from outside, that the outer wall plates tenon into the tie-beams' flanks.

Sturmer, St. Mary The nave roof is of considerable importance being double hammerbeamed, and an example of decadent carpentry which has needed reinforcing with iron tie rods. The pierced tracery panels fitted between hammerbeams and posts, and the rafters, are of poor character and lack Gothic style. The vine-leaf trail is carved round the wall plates, and pendants with foliage carving are affixed to the soffits of the principal collars.

Sutton, All Saints Nave roof in two bays, crown post and seven cants; the crown post is square and chamfered into an irregular octagon with capital and base. The chancel is also roofed in seven cants with a square-sectioned crown post on the central tie beam. The north wall plate of the chancel shows a stop-splayed scarf, probably of the 14th century at the latest. The timber belfry is on two portal frames and has bracing in the first, visible, stage of its turret which suggests the 14th century. The south door is one of the rare type, assembled with counter rebates, see p. 92. Its top and base seem to have been cut off. The south porch is of great interest, and is dated 1633, in the spandrels of a timber single-centred opening, and beneath a strip of 'guilloche' decoration. It has turned baluster-type mullions in each side.

Takeley, Holy Trinity Nave roof with four crown posts of octagonal section, having Perpendicular capitals and bases. There are four braces to each post, and these are treated in the relatively rare manner of an obtuse angle on the inner edge, instead of a radius. The tie beams have double-ogee mouldings, and the wall plates are double-—inner and external, 15th century.

Tendring, St. Edmund King and Martyr The nave roof resembles that at Middleton (q.v.) in that it has raised tie beams, tenoned between its principal rafters. It has queen posts above these ties, raking struts above the collars, side purlins and numerous braces of distinctly Tudor arcuation. Of this roof there are five bays, each of four common rafters. The west bay contains both north and south doors, which are cased on the inside in timber that is traceried and moulded entirely in mid-14th-century style. The hammerbeams

131

mounted above these appear to have been a tie beam, with its central piece removed. For details of these door-cases see Fig. 79, and p. 88.

Terling, All Saints Little timber of age or interest. The chancel has a roof in seven cants, possibly early. The west door, into the base area of the tower (of 1732), has a stone doorway dated by R.C.H.M. to *c.* 1340 and subjected to a resetting, but in this are hung a pair of rather primitive doors, made of V-edged boards, battened, but without a rear frame except round the Decorated curves at their tops.

Thaxted, St. John the Baptist North and south doors with heavy durns, and rear framing rivetted together in portcullis fashion. Their ledges are lapped under the vertical members, and their outer faces are clad with tracery — this tracery is of poor quality, either five- or four-foiled. Nave roof camber-beamed and magnificent, four panels wide, early 16th century. The roof of the north aisle is in 6½ bays with knees and wall pieces at each bay, and angel carvings at the bay centres, believed to date from *c.* 1475. The south aisle has a roof of the early 16th century, well carved with angel figures and heraldry. The south transept roof is dated to the period 1325–50, and is of three trusses; and the northern transept is roofed with a king post and side purlin construction two bays long, which appears to date from either the late 14th, or the early years of the 15th century. The roofs of the north and south chapels have wall pieces and braces; these are both four bays long, and the southern roof is painted, both being of the early 16th century. The chancel roof is of the early 16th century and has short king posts. An important and most rewarding church, unusually rich and varied in Perpendicular carpentry.

Theydon Bois, St. Mary By Smirke and of 1850.

Theydon Garnon, All Saints The nave roof is of great interest, being one of the few having scissor braces combined with crown posts; of which category only four have survived in the county. The crown posts are of cross-quadrate section and the original tie beams are straight and mounted on wall pieces with steeply arched braces. Three bays of this roof, at the east, have chase-tenoned scissors and date the same as do the crown posts; while the two bays at the west have ancient scissors, 11 couples of which can be seen to have open notch-lapped foot-joints. These should date from the early 13th century. The collar purlin and crown posts were evidently carried to the west end at the time of their insertion — for the sake of symmetry.

The north arcade is of six octagonal, oaken piers, dating as does the aisle fabric to 1644, set in bricks in its eastern gable. The wall plates of this arcade are composite and made of beaded-casement mouldings — Perpendicular. The chancel roof is of seven cants; it is ceiled and cannot be seen or dated.

Theydon Mount, St. Michael Built between 1611 and 1614, according to the registers.

Thorpe-le-Soken, St. Michael Much was built by W. White in 1876. The nave roof is ceiled, and only the ends of its diagonal ties are visible; it is the only other roof framed in the same manner as that at Fingringhoe. It has two rows of carved heads on each side. These are difficult to see, it being a poorly-lit nave, but their date may well precede that of the Fingringhoe specimens. North porch has a good timber roof.

Thorrington, St. Mary Magdalene Nave roof with scissor braces and collars, chancel of seven cants; both of pine and of the 19th century. North aisle has a roof of Victorian scissors which lack collars. The west tower has a very good first floor, framed upon two crossed bridging joists, and with a carved Tudor 'rose' in a quatrefoil at the crossing. The bridgers have knees of Tudor arcuation beneath them, but no wall pieces.

Thundersley, St. Peter Nave roof in three bays, crown posts on straight chamfered tie beams, finished in seven cants. The crown posts are quadrate in section, without capitals or bases. The roof of the north aisle appears to be of the same date as does the nave roof, and is of much interest. Both nave and aisles basically early 13th-century. The belfry is good and stands on a complex system of vertical posts.

Tilbury-juxta-Clare, St. Margaret The large, wide nave roof is plastered, and of seven cants. It has tie beams with straight undersides and slightly cambered tops. These are set on wall pieces with knees that are carved with unconvincing tracery. The inner wall plates are moulded in a complex manner, with numerous convex and concave items of different widths. This plate could be of the late 14th century, on this ground. The chancel has a seven cant roof, of that type in which the scissors are made up with many short pieces, all tenoned into the frames—as at Belchamp St. Paul, q.v. (Fig. 35). The south door is in two halves, with central shuts and Decorated arch to its head; it is well framed at the rear with heavy, continuous curved edge members and rivetted crossings of the stiles and ledges. The face planks have humped surfaces, and the front mouldings are cymas and filletted rounds. The south porch has a deep, crenellated, Perpendicular wall plate and a roof of seven common couples framed into seven cants.

Tillingham, St. Nicholas Contains no timber earlier than 19th century.

Tilty, St. Mary the Virgin The chancel has a high, plastered roof in seven cants the wall plate of which is visible and contemporary, i.e. 14th century.

Tiptree, St. Luke 1855 by E. Christian.

Tollesbury, St. Mary All Victorian timber.

Tolleshunt D'Arcy, St. Nicholas The chancel roof is crown post and seven cants, and is ascribed by the author of the local guide to *c.* 1450; the cross-section of the crown post is quatrefoil with fillets on, and between each roll (foil). South door of Decorated arcuation with good fully-dovetailed rear frame and moulded front members. Illustrated in Fig. 81 on p. 91.

Tolleshunt Knights, All Saints The nave roof in three bays, with tie beams on wall pieces having solid hanging knees beneath them; rafters above framed into seven cants by chase tenons. The inner wall plate and tie beams have a unique moulding, with a large and small hollow divided by two beak arrises of the Decorated period. The north door also Decorated, with V-edged planks and strap hinges. Redundant, now vested in Greek Orthodox Church.

Tolleshunt Major, St. Nicholas Nave roof of seven cants with one crown post on a cambered central tie beam. South porch curious and unconvincing, apparently created by the Rev. E. Geldart in 1888. There is a tie beam to the chancel roof, with double-ogee soffit-corner chamfers apparently of the mid-15th century. There are remains of a timber belfry in the west end of the nave, which was formerly on two portal frames of which only the transoms remain. The collar purlin is properly framed into the east wall of the turret's lower stage, and is therefore contemporary.

Toppesfield, St. Margaret of Antioch Nave and chancel roofs in seven cants and plastered. Church locked and this observation made through a clear glass window. North porch with king-post roof and Perpendicular chamfers visible, formerly fitted with clasping mullions, and traceried side planks.

Twinstead, St. John the Evangelist 1860 'in the style of Butterfield'.

Ugley, St. Peter 1866, of little interest.

Ulting, All Saints The nave roof is built in two bays; it is tied at the chancel division, open and arched to the collars at the centre, and tied again at the west end, where the beam supports the belfry. The central arched-collar frame is illustrated in Fig. 22, in view of its general interest, and dating.

Upminster, St. Laurence The most interesting carpentry here, in fact the main interest of the church, is the spire frame which is illustrated in Plate XXII. This is jointed with secret notched lap joints, and dates from the closing years of the 13th century. It is described more fully under 'Belfries' on pp. 62-3. The remainder of the church is largely of 1862 and by W. G. Bartlett.

Upshire, St. Thomas 1902 by Freeman & Ogilvy, timber nave arcade.

Vange, All Saints Locked, and with keys that are elusive. Nave roof is crown post as may be seen through the clear glass windows; the posts have four braces, and the tie beams are chamfered. There are inner and outer wall plates, and it can be seen that the rafters are stopped on the upper faces of the soles. Date uncertain, but early.

Virley, St. Mary A ruin of great character, but no timbers survive.

Wakes Colne, All Saints The north porch has fine verge boards, but has otherwise been much restored. North door has V-edged planks affixed to cross battens with no proper frame at rear. The nave roof is of seven cants, ceiled, but one wall piece is left visible. It is finely carved with cymas and hollows and may well indicate the existence of a fine roof. The west belfry was restored in the 15th century.

Waltham Abbey, Holy Cross What survives as the parish church is the nave and aisles of the former abbey, as rebuilt during the early years of the 12th century. It seems that, until the beginning of the 19th century, it had retained a roof of the same age, but this was cut about and rehashed into a king-post and raking-strut system; signed with 'LTW, CP, 1807', doubtless by its makers. The timbers re-used for this were all notch-lapped, in a manner well suited to a c. 1130 ascription (see page 6).

Walthamstow, St. Mary Not examined, endless rebuildings having taken place, culminating in that of 1843.

Walton on Naze, All Saints 1873–82 by H. Stone.

Wanstead, St. Mary 1790 by T. Hardwick. Not seen.

Weeley, St. Andrew Allegedly 1881, by E. C. Robins.

Wendens Ambo, St. Mary the Virgin South porch with roof in seven cants, crown post, 14th century. In the nave only the tie beams and wall plates are of interest, all the above dating from some restoration.

Wennington, St. Mary and St. Peter Nave roof crown post and seven cants, plastered. Chancel also in seven cants; a good door in the east end of the south aisle.

West Bergholt, St. Mary Both nave and chancel roofs in seven cants, plastered over, and possibly dating from the major rebuilding of *c.* 1300. The western belfry is of two builds, the earlier during the 14th century. This incorporates a lodged floor made from timbers that apparently came from an earlier timber western structure that closed this end of the Saxon nave. This fact became evident when the church was examined and excavated recently, and it was found to have been an enlargement of a single cell Saxon church, with apsidal eastern end, and no masonry west end—the excavator assessed this as *c.* A.D. 1000. The re-used timbers were the angle posts of a tower-type structure and show open notched lap joints that may prove the origin of that type to have been pre-Conquest.

West Hanningfield, St. Mary and St. Edward The south porch is very interesting, see Fig. 47. South door also of interest, and west door into the belfry. Nave roof crown post with seven cants heavily plastered and obscured, but certainly four braces to each post—14th century or earlier. The west belfry is the fascinating part of this church, built on four vertical posts, having one trefoil tracery surviving and a carved mask in the first-floor framing.

West Mersea, St. Peter and St. Paul The chancel roof is arched to its collars, with numerous double-ogee mouldings and rather flattened arcuation—indicative of the Perpendicular period. This roof has only one internal wall plate and its pitch is almost as low as 45°. The date of the west tower is uncertain: late Saxon, Norman or the Saxo-Norman 'overlap'; it has blocked Romanesque windows visible internally, in the upper stage. The first floor is of joists and trimmers that have 'free tenons' on their *ends*—a most unusual technique. The floor under the bell chamber is largely original, although reinforced in *c.* 1900. This was formerly mounted upon wall posts that have left traces in the plastered walls; its joists show chase mortises with sunken butment cheeks made to receive spur-shouldered chase tenons. This might prove such joints to date earlier than at Bradwell-juxta-Coggeshall. In the bell chamber some very heavy timbers were re-used to mount the frames, and these may be of very great age.

Wethersfield, St. Mary Magdalene and St. Mary the Virgin The most significant piece of carpentry in this church, historically, is the framing of the spire, which is illustrated in Fig. 55. This is of the close of the 13th century and incorporates four notched lap joints. The frame is profusely saltire-braced, and is evidence as to the period during which the separate traditions of straight and bent-wood usage began to combine in this county.
    The door into the tower stair is contemporary with the masonry, as is the samson post placed in the centre of the ground floor to support the first floor. Early 13th century. The south door of the church is of interest and good quality. It is of Decorated arcuation having a cheaply jointed rear frame of portcullis pattern, well planed edge moulding on its face planks,

and good strap hinges. The north door is also good and similar.

Nave roof is camberbeamed and has a ridge piece, with a butt purlin in each slope; it is in four bays, and has wall pieces with Tudor-style pendant ends, resting on wooden corbels.

White Colne, St. Andrew   Restored, 1869 by C. J. Moxon. Nave roofed with 18 couples, in seven cants, which may well have survived the restoration.

White Notley, St. Etheldreda   One of the most interesting churches in the county, as far as carpentry is concerned. The nave roof bears little relation, chronologically, to the dates of the masonry of the north and south aisles. It is, however, a good roof, spoilt by plastering. Framed in seven cants with tie beams on wall pieces with arch braces, the latter form four-centred arches and have void spandrels. The wall piece nearest the chancel arch is carved into a crenellated, terminal form, at its lower end; no supporting corbel exists and it is a pendant by definition. The mouldings of all the timbers are nondescript, and could occur at any time during the Perpendicular period. The timber belfry at the west end is dated by the local information board to between 1485 and 1509, the reign of Henry VII. This belfry is illustrated in Fig. 62 on p. 71. The date to which the belfry is ascribed assists with the dating of the nave roof, since it cannot be shown that either was built independently of the other. A thorough examination inside the base of the turret indicated that they were contemporaries. The chancel roof is of seven cants, in 20 couples, with some panels inserted between the ashlars; it may date from last restoration of the chancel. The south aisle is ascribed (L.G.B.) to *c.* 1250 and possesses an unusual lean-to roof with good head carvings on its main sole pieces. This could date as early as the 14th century. The north aisle is different in that its lean-to roof is mounted on wall pieces, and the inner wall plates tenoned into them. The south porch is a good example, and of 14th-century origin (illustrated in Fig. 41). The south door is also of this century.

White Roding, St. Martin   The nave roof is probably the most interesting of its kind in the county, since it incorporates some very early repair work, and this is helpful in ascertaining the date of the type of couples then inserted. It is a crown-post roof with plain, square crown posts that are downward braced to the tie beams, which are very slightly cambered and have chamfered lower arrises. The wall plates are double and carry inclined ashlar pieces. Perhaps the most significant feature is the scarf used to unite the two pieces of collar purlin — a trait-de-Jupiter. This helps to date the roof, probably to the period 1250–1300. One western bay was repaired, probably during the early 14th century, when double collars were introduced with a second, high, collar purlin. The seven cants are formed by the scissor braces which are, in this example, trenched through the collars (see Fig. 9).

The chancel roof is similar, crown post with seven cants, due to trenched scissors. The tie beam is set on wall pieces with arch braces having void, but very small, spandrels. The crown post is octagonal, with capital and base treatment which should be of Perpendicular date — perhaps mid-14th century, but unlikely to be later; the posts seem cleaner, and newer than the rafters.

The south door is Norman, and is illustrated in Fig. 67. It is a rare example, and its age is uncertain, because other Norman doors which have survived are constructed in different ways (see description on p. 79).

Wicken Bonhunt, St. Margaret Largely 1858–59, by J. H. Sperling. The chancel has a roof in seven cants, which is ceiled, and unexaminable. This could date, as does the chancel, to the 13th century.

Wicken Bonhunt, Chapel of St. Helen None of the roof timber shows notched-lap matrices, nor any sign of re-use. Roof date therefore uncertain, but not of much interest.

Wickham Bishops The old church, in ruins and dangerous, has a chancel roof in seven cants with tie beams on wall pieces with solid knees. The wall plate is of *c.* 1475.

Wickham St. Paul, All Saints Nave roof ceiled with plasterboard, but framed into seven cants, and having tie beams mounted on wall pieces with three hollow mouldings; their braces are of Tudor arcuation and late 15th century. The tower, of 1505, has a dated valley roof, supported on a heavy beam.

Widdington, St. Mary Only the south door seems to pre-date the rebuilding of 1872. This has a full-dovetailed rear frame and is in two halves with central shuts. The front has humped planks and hollow-chamfered face fillets.

Widford, St. Mary 1862 by St. Aubyn.

The Willingales, Doe and Spain, St. Christopher Restored south porch, embodying a re-used crown post. The chancel roof has early sole pieces with the rafters tenoned into their upper faces.

The Willingales, St. Andrew Contains remains of a portal-frame belfry, with cusped braces to its eastern transom. The turret is very largely replacement, and of little interest. The north door mounts some good iron work of the 12th century.

Wimbish, cum Thunderley, All Saints The roof of the Norman nave is both rare and important, being scissor-braced, the scissors in trenches with tenoned ends — late 13th century. The wall plates are very elaborately moulded, and are tenoned into the tie beams, which are closely spaced with only three or four rafters between them. The north aisle roof is flat, with central purlin, wall pieces and traceried spandrel knees — one dated 1534, in curious figures.

Witham, St. Nicholas A largely 14th-century church, with what might be its 14th-century roofing, throughout. Nave roof, too high for examination, of seven cants. North and south aisles are crown post with collar purlin.

Wivenhoe, St. Mary the Virgin Mainly by Hakewill in 1860.

Woodford, St. Mary the Virgin Mainly 1817, by C. Begon.

Woodham Ferrers, St. Mary the Virgin An interesting building, the dates of which are known — between *c.* 1250 and *c.* 1330. The south porch is good, a timber one with crown-post roof and cinque-foil side lights — mid- to late 15th century. Nave roof is scissor-braced, the scissors trenched and with tenoned ends — late 13th century. The inner wall plate is scroll moulded. The west bay contains a timber belfry that is built on two beams without wall pieces or posts. The north aisle roof is canted, and framed with purlins and principals, both moulded with hollows and rounds in profusion — 14th century. Chancel roof in seven cants, with moulded inner wall plate. The local information ascribes this chancel to *c.* 1290. The south door is of the

15th century, with hollow-moulded face fillets and a rear frame assembled by square-ended lap joints and much heavy iron work.

Wormingford, St. Andrew The nave roof is one of the most ambitious in the county of its date—19th century. It is of resinous soft wood and has thin panels of pierced tracery in abundance. North aisle roof is camberbeam.

Wrabness, All Saints With a single hammerbeam roof over the nave, the hammerbeams are mounted on knees with leaf-carved faces. All mouldings are Perpendicular. The chancel roof is dated by the parochial register for the year 1687, in which the chancel collapsed. It was replaced by a roof of seven cants, however, or had its old roof put back on. This point cannot be decided because the timbers and their jointing cannot be seen, due to a ceiling.

Writtle, All Saints Both porches are of interest. The south porch has a gambrel roof of c. 1440–50. That on the north has a simple roof of seven cants, with mouldings which indicate the period 1475–1500. The nave roof is datable to the building of the clerestory—c. 1470–80. It is a very good camberbeam specimen with wall pieces and bosses. Both north and south aisle roofs are contemporary with that of the nave. The chancel has a roof of seven cants, which was, according to the guide for visitors, panelled and boarded at the same time as the clerestory was raised.

GLOSSARY

Addorsed: From heraldry, meaning placed back to back—the opposite of 'addressed', or face to face.

Angle tie: Tying timbers placed across angles, normally the returns of wall plates. These were widely used during the 18th century as a means to step hip rafters, which were seated in a third timber, the dragon piece.

Abutment: *Abut*, O.Fr. *abuter*, to touch at the end (*à*, to, *bout*, end). Any point in timber jointing where one timber's end touches another constitutes an abutment. A 'butt-joint' is, therefore, one where ends meet; no integration is implied.

Anglo-Norman Romanesque: A period of English architectural history during which the style was based on Roman buildings having round, or single centred arches, covering the period from the Conquest in 1066 until *c*.1200.

Anglo-Saxon Romanesque: The period of English architectural history covering the years between *c*.1000 and the Norman Conquest in 1066.

Arcature: The curvature of an arch, as segmental, ogee or lancet.

Arcade: A range of arches. Term applied also to the series of posts standing inside an aisled timber building, because they are sometimes arch-braced in their longitudinal direction.

Arch braces: Term generally applied to braces beneath tie beams, which were frequently curved, or arched.

Arris: The edge at which two surfaces meet.

Arris-trenched: Trenched (q.v.), so that the trench is cut obliquely through an arris and affects both adjacent surfaces.

Ashlar pieces: Short, vertical timbers at the feet of rafters, generally standing upon sole pieces. These continue the internal wall surface until it meets the underside of the rafters, avoiding a visual discontinuity and greatly strengthening the rafters' base.

Barefaced: With the face uncovered, without a mask; avowed, open. Term used to denote a timber joint possessed of only one shoulder, but which normally possesses two.

Base crucks: Timbers placed as wall posts and containing the naturally grown angle of the eaves, above which they may rise to collar height.

Bays: The divisions, normally postulated by the material used for construction of the lengths of buildings. In the case of arcades, each arch is taken as one bay.

Bird's-mouth: Term used to describe joints bearing a visual resemblance to an open bird's beak.

Blade, -ing, -ed: Term used to specify scarfs that are face-halved and terminated in inset, barefaced tongues.

Bole: The butt of a tree trunk, normally of concave conoid form, used to provide jowls by inverting the timber.

Bowtell: Small roll moulding, or bead.

Brace: Any timber reinforcing an angle, usually subjected to compression.

Bridle: Term applied to timber joints having open-ended mortises and tenons resembling a horse's mouth with the bit of the bridle in place.

Bridle-butted scarf: That category of scarf, or end-to-end joints for timbers which was in use throughout the Perpendicular period. An example is shown in Fig. 23.

Bressummer: Breast-summer, a timber extending for the length of a timber building, normally forming the sill of a jettied storey.

Bridging-joist: Floor timber that supports the ends of common joists, and normally bridges the bays from one binding-joist to the next.

Broach: A spit or point.

Butment cheeks: The timber left on either side of mortises, against which the shoulders of tenons abut.

Butts: The ends of jointed timbers, or those parts of the edges of timbers touched by ends, and constituting abutments.

Butt-joints: The category of timber joints in which neither piece penetrates the other. When assembled the components merely touch, without any integration. They are held in contact by other timbers, or irons.

Butt-notches. Type of jointing for timbers which is shown at 'a' in Fig. 3. The notch is the nick, or indentation formed by the two converging cuts in the face of one timber, and the butt is the suitably shaped end of the other timber. These joints can only resist compression, and are archaic.

Camber beams: Beams sufficiently cambered to form the basis of the simplest type of roof, their curvature serving to drain their surfaces when clad.

Cant: The oblique line or surface which cuts off the corner of a square or cube. The term is applied to soulaces in roofs, because they produce a canted plane; roofs possessing soulaces, collars and ashlar pieces are thus described as 'of seven cants'.

Cant post: Posts that converge upwards; see Navestock belfry.

Chamfer: The slope or bevel created by removing a timber's corner or arris. These are termed 'through' if run off the end of the workpiece, 'stopped' if terminating in a decorative form before the end of the piece or its conjunction with another.

Chase: From *chasse*, a shrine for relics. In carpentry a score cut length-wise, a lengthened hollow, groove, or furrow.

Chase, or chased mortise: A long mortise into which a tenon may be inserted sidewise.

Chase-tenon: a tenon which can be inserted into its (chase-) mortise in two ways, lengthwise or laterally. Two such tenons are shown in Fig. 7 on the sole- and ashlar-piece.

Cladding: The external covering applied to a wall or a roof.

Clamp: A term applied variously to timbers depending upon the type of building. In houses the term denotes horizontal timbers attached to the wall studs in order to support floors; these clamps normally indicate the later intrusion of such floors.

Clench, clinch: Either to turn the point of a nail or spike, and re-drive it back into the timber through which it has passed; or to form its end into a rivet, or clench, by beating it out upon a washer or rove.

140

Coak: A peg or dowel of a diameter almost equal to its length, used in 19th-century shipwrighting to join futtocks and timbers because it was cheaper than scarfing them.

Cogging: A method of housing an entire timber's end, sometimes used to prevent its rotation—as in door cases.

Collar: A horizontal member placed across a rafter-couple, between their base and their apex, and considered to be in compression, normally. An example is shown at lower right in Fig. 5.

Collar beam: A roof timber, placed horizontally and uniting a rafter couple at a point between the bases and the apex. Collar beams can act either as ties or strainers.

Collar-purlin: A lengthwise timber in a roof assembly, of which an example is shown in Fig. 9. It is carried by vertical crown-posts, and connects the successive rafter-couples, longitudinally, by their collars. Its purpose was the lengthwise stability of the whole roof.

Compass timber: A term denoting timber of natural and grown curvature, as distinct from relatively straight-grown timber from which curves are cut.

Common joist, -rafter: The majority of either kind, and normally those of the least cross section in any floor or roof.

Corner post: The post standing at the return of two walls, as at the end and adjacent side of a building.

Counter rebate: See Fig. 57.

Crenellate: To furnish with battlements, a decorative device used much in timber buildings.

Crown-post: Vertical timber posts, much carved and decorated in Perpendicular times (see Fig. 15), and plain functional posts at their inception, as shown in Fig. 9. These stood, normally, upon tie-beams and carried the collar-purlin.

Cruck blade: The elbowed timber forming one half of a pair of crucks.

Cusp: In Gothic tracery the pointed shape or form created by the intersection of two concave arcs.

Cyma: Ogee. Formed by a concave and a convex arc in a single linear association.

Decorated, period: That period of English architectural history covering the years between *c.* 1250/1350.

Dormer: An upright window protruding from the pitch of a roof.

Double tenons: Two tenons cut from the same timber's end and placed in line; if side by side they constitute a pair of single tenons.

Dragon beam, -piece: A timber bisecting the angle formed by two wall plates. If a beam it supports a jetty continued around the angle; if a piece it normally serves to step a hip rafter.

Draw knife, or -shave: A hand tool possessing handles at either end of its blade, used to produce chamfers.

Durns: Timbers with grown bends suitable for the manufacture of door-ways of Gothic arcatures; two were frequently sawn from one piece of the requisite form.

Early English, period: That part of our architectural history approximating to *c.* 1150-1250.

Eaves: The underside of a roof's pitch that projects outside a wall.

End girt, -girth: Horizontal timber in an end wall placed halfway betwixt top plate and groundsill, thereby shortening the studs and stiffening the wall.

Fascia: A board forming a front, frequently used to cover a number of timbers' ends, as joists at a jetty, or rafters at an eaves.

Fillet: In moulding profiles a small raised band, normally of square section. Also a small squared timber.

Fish: A length of timber with tapering ends which can be used to cover and strengthen a break in another timber.

Fished scarf: A scarf that relies upon the introduction of a third timber.

Footing: Foundation.

Free tenon: A tenon used as a separate item, both ends being fitted into mortises cut into two timbers to be joined; often used to effect edge-to-edge joints.

Gambrel: Perhaps Old French (Norman). 'Also gambrel roof . . . so called from its resemblance to the shape of a horse's hind leg' (*O.E.D.*, 1933).

Girth, girt: Horizontal timbers in wall frames, placed at half height, which shorten and thereby stiffen the studs.

Groundsill: The first horizontal timber laid for a timber building. As the name implies these were in ancient times laid directly upon the ground, as was the case at Greensted church, Essex.

Halving: In jointing the removal of half the thicknesses of two timbers, as in cross halving.

Harr, arr: The edge timber of a door leaf or gate nearest the hinges, the opposite edge timber of which is the head.

Hanging knee: Term denoting a knee placed beneath a beam. Knees placed above beams are 'standing knees, or standards', and those in the horizontal plane are 'lodging knees'. All three derive from shipwrighting and were used in ships as early as the Viking period.

Haunch: Adjuncts of tenons, designed to resist winding; they may be square or diminished.

Header: Short timber to carry rafters' tops at the exiture of chimney-stacks.

Hewn knee: A knee, or angle, cut from a timber's end, as distinct from a separate and applied piece.

Hip rafter: A rafter pitched on the line of intersection of two inclined planes of roof, forming the arris of a pyramidal form.

Hogging: Stress caused by supporting the centre of a beam and leaving the ends unsupported, as when a wave rises amidships of a vessel, and beneath her.

Housing: In jointing a cavity large enough to hold an entire timber's end.

Jacobean: The period between 1603 and 1625—the reign of James I.

Jamb: The side of a doorway, archway or window.

Jetty: The projection of a floor outside its substructure, upon which the next storey was built. This resulted in floor areas that increased as the storeys ascended.

Joggle: Said of two timbers, both of which enter a third but which have their joints out of line in order to avoid excessive weakening.

Joist: The horizontal timbers supporting floors; these are binding, bridging, common and trimming. Binders unite storey posts; bridgers span or bridge each bay from binder to binder; commons are the most numerous and actually carry the floor boards. Trimmers are used to frame the edges of voids, such as stair wells.

Jowl: (Jole) 'The external throat or neck when fat or prominent ... the dewlap of cattle'. (*O.E.D.*) Term applied to the thickened ends of such timbers as storey posts which facilitate the jointing of several other timbers.

Kerf: The cut produced by a saw.

Key: Tapered piece of dense hardwood transfixing a scarf, used to close its abutments.

King stud: A stud placed centrally in a gable, normally supporting the collar purlin.

Lap dovetail: That form of dovetail that overlaps, and is not finished flush. The alternative form is the 'through dovetail' used by cabinet makers; they may also be 'secret', 'secret-mitred' or double.

Lap joints: Any jointed timbers which overlap each other.

Lodged: 'To put and cause to remain in a specified place.' (*O.E.D.*) A term applied to floors retained in place by their weight alone.

Main span: In aisled buildings this is the central and greatest distance spanned.

Midstrey: The porch-like structure at the front of a barn, derived from middle-strey. Each bay of a barn was a strey, and ancient barns normally had one such porch at their centre.

Mitre: Abutments at 45 degrees, producing square returns.

Muntins: Vertical members of panelled areas; the term may derive from mountants.

Mullions: Vertical components of windows, placed in the void.

Nogging: The material used to infill a framed wall betwixt sill and top.

Notched laps: A category of lap joints having V-shaped indentations on plan-view to prevent their lengthwise withdrawal.

Outshot, outshut: An area of space added to a building's bays, normally at the sides: when at the end of a building they are called by the ancient term 'culatia'.

Passing brace: A brace uniting several successive members of a frame and passing them by means of halved jointing; of mainly Early English and Decorated usage. (Author's coinage, 1962, without historical validity.)

Perpendicular period: That part of English architectural history covering, approximately, 1350-1450.

Plate: A horizontal timber laid at the base of a timber frame; the term implies a footing, as distinct from a groundsill.

Prebend: The share of the revenues of a cathedral or collegiate church allowed to a clergyman who officiates in it at stated times.

Prick post: Any vertical timber placed in compression, but not a storey post.

Principal-rafter: A heavy rafter placed at bay intervals, normally associated with side purlins.

Purlin: A longitudinal timber in a roof.

Queen posts: Posts set in pairs between tie beams and collars and acting in compression.

Raking struts: Inclined struts used in pairs between tie beams and principal-rafters.

Reversed-assembly: Indicates a system of rearing transverse framing units, the lengthwise timbers of which (top plates) are laid last. In these cases the tie beams are *under* the top plates. (Author's coinage, 1962, without historical validity.)

Rive: To split timber lengthwise, i.e. along its grain.

Rove: The circular plate, or washer, upon which the clench, or rivet, in boat- or ship-building is formed.

Sagging: Stress caused by supporting the ends of a timber and applying weight to its centre.

Sally: An obtusely angular and pointed projection, normally on a timber's end. Alternatively a 'tace'.

Samson post: 'Pillar erected in a ship's hold, between the lower deck and the Kelson'. (*O.E.D.*) The term alludes to the strength of Samson (Judges XVI, 29), and is applied to similar posts used to support early floors.

Scarfing: The jointing of relatively short timbers into continuous lengths, by means of various expedients; the four faces are smooth and continuous.

Scarfed cruck: A cruck blade having a scarf-jointed angle, as distinct from a grown angle.

Scissor-braces: Timbers crossed in a saltire and connecting a pair of rafters, illustrated in Fig. 3, at 'b'.

Secret notched-lap: A development of the notched lap-joint, in which the notch itself cannot be seen, since covered by a flange of timber. An example of the socket cut to receive one of these is shown in Fig. 7, where it is the third joint from the base of the rafter shown at the right.

Set: The divergence of the sides of a dovetail.

Seven-cants: The seven short, straight sides of the partial polygon built into certain timber roofs. Both 'a' and 'b' examples shown in Fig. 3 have seven cants. Such frames have been called 'trussed-rafters' during the last century.

Shore: An inclined timber supporting a vertical one, acting in compression.

Shuts: The edges of a door leaf collectively form the 'shuts' of that door.

Side girt, girth: See end girt.

Soffit: Underside or archivolt.

Sole pieces: Short horizontal timbers forming the base of any raftering system that has a base triangulation.

Soulace: A definitive term (Salzman, 1952) for secondary timbers connecting rafters with collars, and placed *under* the latter.

Splayed-scarf: A scarf, or end-to-end timber joint, which is effected by diminishing both ends to either nothing, or to a butt. An example is shown at lower left in Fig. 8.

Spur tie: A short tie such as connects a cruck blade and a wall plate, or a collar arch and a wall plate.

Spire mast: Central vertical timber of a framed spire.

Squint: Angle other than 90 degrees.

Storey post: A wall post of a multi-storeyed timber building that continues through the floor levels.

Straining beam: A horizontal beam between two posts, acting in compression to keep them apart.

Strut: A timber in a roof system that acts in compression, in a secondary capacity.

Stub tenon: A short tenon that does not entirely penetrate the mortised concomitant timber.

Studs: From O.E. *studu*, a post; the vertical common timbers of framed timber walls.

Table: A raised rectangular portion on a worked timber, normally a scarf adjunct.

Tace: See sally.

Tail: The male part of a dovetail joint.

Tie beams: Beams laid across buildings to tie both walls together; they must have unwithdrawable end joints for this purpose.

Tongue: A fillet worked along the edge of a plank to enter a groove in another.

Top plate: A horizontal timber along the top of a framed wall.

Trait-de-Jupiter: The early form of scarf-joint which is shown in Fig. 9; so named in medieval times because of its visual resemblance to lightning, or the zig-zag.

Transom: A cross beam acting as a support for the superstructure.

Trench: A square sectioned groove cut across the grain.

Trussed, Truss: In roof-framing trusses are the most rigid and stable frames, such as those having tie-beams in Fig. 9. Main-frames would be a more defensible term, however.

Tusk: The wooden key driven through the protruding end of a tusked tenon, an unwithdrawable form of that joint.

Waney: Used to describe timber, the squared section of which is the greatest that can be cut from the rounded trunk, when any missing sharp arrises are said to be 'waney' edges.

Winding: In carpentry the result of torque or twisting, or the result of drying a spirally-grained tree.

Wind braces: Braces fitted into the angles of either roofs or walls to resist wind pressures.

Only terms that are likely to be strange to the general reader are here given, and the correct reference is, of course, the *Oxford English Dictionary*.

BIBLIOGRAPHY

Arnold, T., *Memorials of St. Edmund's Abbey*, Rolls series, 96 (London, 1890).

Barker, F., ed. and trans., *Vita Aedwardi Regis* (London, 1890).

Beaumont, G. F., *A History of Coggeshall in Essex* (London, 1890).

Berger, R., ed., *Scientific Contributions to Medieval Archaeology* (1970).

Bilson, J., 'Notes on the earlier Architectural History of Wells Cathedral', *Archaeological Journal* (1928).

Boustred, R., and Trace, K., *The Parish Church of St. Ouen*, Colchester, 1969.

Brown, G. Baldwin, *The Arts in Early England II, Anglo-Saxon Architecture* (London, 1903. 2nd ed. 1925).

Bruce-Mitford, R. L. S., *The Sutton Hoo Ship Burial* (B.M. Trustees, London, 1954).

The Builder, Vol. LXXXVII (1904).

Calendar of Patent Rolls, Vol. II, Edward VI (H.M.S.O.).

Cave, P., *Hospital of St. Cross* (1970).

Chapman, F. R., ed., *The Sacrist Rolls of Ely*, Vol. I (Cambridge, 1907).

Chisenhall-Marsh, T. C., *Domesday Book, relating to Essex* (Chelmsford, 1864).

Christensen, A. E., jnr., *Vikingskipene* (Oslo, 1970).

Chubb, Rev. N., *All Saints, Brixworth* (1977).

Clapham, A. W., *English Romanesque Architecture, After the Conquest* (1964).

Clowes, G. S. Laird, *Sailing Ships, their History and Development* (H.M.S.O., 1932).

Colchester, L. S. and Harvey, Dr. J. H., 'Wells Cathedral', *Arch. Jnl.*, Vol. 131 (1974).

Colchester, L. S., *Wells Cathedral Library* (1978) 2nd ed.

Colvin, H. M., ed., *History of the King's Works* (1963).

Cristie, H., Olsen, O. and Taylor H. M., 'The Wooden Church of St. Andrew at Greensted, Essex', *Antiquaries Journal* (1979), Vol. LIX, part I.

Davey, Dr. N., *A History of Building Materials* (London, 1961).

Davis, R. H. C., 'The Norman Conquest', *Hist. Ass. Jnl.*, Vol. LI (1966).

Deneux, H., *Centre Recherches sur les Monuments Historiques*, numerous volumes.

Deneux, H., 'L'Evolution des Charpentes du xie au xve siècle' (C.R.M.H.).

Downes, K., *Hawksmoor* (1969).

Drinkwater, N., 'Old Deanery at Salisbury', *Antiquaries Journal*, 44 (1964).

Dugdale, W., *Monasticon Anglicanum* (London, 1718).

Everett, C. R., 'Notes on the Decanal and other houses in the Close of Sarum', *Wiltshire Archaeological & Natural History Magazine*, 50 (1944).

Finn, R. Welldon, 'Changes in the Population of Essex', *Essex Archaeol./Historical Society*, Vol. 4 (1972).

Fletcher, Sir Banister, *History of Architecture* (1956).

Fletcher, Dr. J., and Haslop, F. W. O., 'The West Range at Ely and its Romanesque Roof', *Archaeological Journal*, vol. 126, 1970.

Forrester, H., *Medieval Gothic Mouldings* (Chichester, 1972).

Gethyn-Jones, Canon D., *Kempley* (1957). Available at the church.

Gibb, J. H., *Sherborne Abbey* (1972).

Grüber, Professor, *Jarbuch der Technischen Hochschule*, Aachen, 1941.

Hale, Archdeacon W. H., *The Domesday of St. Paul's* (Camden Society, 1858).

Hart, C., 'The Site of Assandun', *History Studies*, 1971.

Harvey, Dr. J. H., 'The King's Chief Carpenters', *Arch. Jnl.*, 3rd series, Vol. XI (1948).

Harvey, Dr. J. H., *The Master Builders* (London, 1971).

Harvey, Dr. J. H., *The Perpendicular Style* (1978).

Harvey, Dr. J. H., *English Cathedrals* (1961).

Harvey, Dr. J. H., *The Medieval Architect* (1972).

Harwell, Berkshire Carbon 14/Tritium Dating Laboratory. Certificate dated 2 March 1976. HAR—1258. Age bp (yrs) 1020±90, bp — 1950, 930.

Hewett, C. A., 'The Barns at Cressing Temple, Essex', *Journal of Society of Architectural Historians*, March 1967, Vol. XXVI, No. 1. (U.S.A.).

Hewett, C. A., 'The Dating of French Timber Roofs', *Transactions*, Ancient Monuments Society, new series, Vol. 16 (1969).

Hewett, C. A., and Smith, J. R., 'Faked Masonry of the Mid-13th Century at Navestock Church', *Essex Journal* (1972), pp. 82-85.

Hewett, C. A., 'The Carpentry', *Archaeology in the City of London*, No. 3 (1975).

Hewett, C. A., 'Aisled Timber Halls and Related Buildings, Chiefly in Essex', *Transactions*, Ancient Monuments Society, Vol. 21 (1976).

Hewett, C. A., *English Historic Carpentry*, Chichester, 1980.

Hewett, C. A. and Tatton-Brown, T., *Archaeologia Cantiana*, Vol. XCII.

Highfield, Dr. J. R. L., 'The Aula Custodis', *Postmaster*, Vol. IV, No. 4 (1970).

Hope-Taylor, B., (ed. by C. A. R. Rawley-Radford), 'The Saxon House, A Review and Some Parallels', *Med. Arch.*, No. 1. (1975).

Hunt, E. M., *The History of Ware* (Hertford, 1949).

Jervis, S., *The Woodwork of Winchester Cathedral* (Friends of Win. Cath., 1976).

Kent, Rev. J. A. P., *History of Selby Abbey* (London, 1968).

Kent, W., *The George Inn, Southwark* (1970).

Kidson, Dr. P., *A History of English Architecture* (1965).

Larking, L., *The Knights Hospitallers in England* (Camden Soc., 1857).

Leeds, E. T., *Early Anglo-Saxon Art and Archaeology* (Oxford, 1936).

Lingpen, A. R., ed., *Master Worsley's Book* (London, 1910).

McHardy, A. K., *The Church in London,1375-1392* (London Record Society, 1977).

Mills, D., *Lambeth Palace* (Church Information Board, 1956).

Møller, E., *Traebygningskunsten*.

Morant, P., *History and Antiquities of Essex* (London, 1768, Chelmsford, 1816).

Morgan, F. C., *A Short History of Abbey Dore* (1949-51).

Ogborn, M. E., *Staple Inn* (Institute of Actuaries, 1964).

Parsons, D., ed., *Tenth-Century Studies* (Chichester, 1975).

Pevsner, Sir N., *An Outline of European Architecture* (1943, 1963, 1973).

Pevsner, Sir N., *Buildings of England, Essex*, 1954.

Pevsner, Sir N., *Buildings of England, Suffolk,* 1961.

Postan, M. M., *The Mediaeval Economy and Society* (1972).

Rackham, O., Blair, W. J. and Munby, J. T., *Med. Arch.*, Vol. XXII (1978).

Ray, Rev. P. W., *History of Greensted Church* (Ongar, 1869).

Repton, J. A., *Norwich Cathedral* (Farnborough, 1965).

Reuter, R., *Denkmalpflege*, M5078 F.

Rickman, T. H., 'The Farmhouse, Thorpeacre, Loughborough', *Med. Arch.*, Vol. 12, (1968).

Rigold, S. E., 'Romanesque Bases, in and South-East of the Limestone Belt', *Antiquaries Journal*, Occasional Papers.

Rodwell, Dr. W., 'The Archaeological Investigation of Hadstock Church, Essex', *Antiquaries Journal*, Vol. LVI, part I (1976).

Royal Commission on Historic Monuments, Inventory, Essex, 1926. (H.M.S.O.).

Rudder, S., *A New History of Gloucestershire* (1779).

Saeftel, Dr. F., *Krummholz und cruck-Dachwerke in Nordwest-Europa*, Eckenforde, 1970.

Salzman, L., *Building in England* (1952).

Sherley-Price, L., trans., *A History of the English Church and People* (1968).

Simpson, Sir J. W., *Some Account of the Old Hall of Lincoln's Inn* (Brighton, 1928).

Stenton, Sir F., *English Families and the Conquest* (1968).

Stranks, Ven. C. J., *Durham Cathedral* (London, 1971).

Taylor, Dr. H. M. and J., *Anglo-Saxon Architecture* (Cambridge, 1965).

Teledyne Isotopes, 50 Van Buren Avenue, Westwood, New Jersey, 07675. Dated 11 December 1978.

Isotopes Number 1-10, 488. $\dfrac{-\delta\ C^{14}}{112\pm9}$ $\dfrac{\text{Age in years B.P.}}{995\pm80}$

Thorpe, B., *The Anglo-Saxon Chronicle* trans. Longman, Green (London, 1861).

Victoria County History of Essex (London, 1956).

Whitham, J. A., *The Church of St. Mary of Ottery* (1968).

Wilson, C. G., *Winchester Cathedral Record* (Friends of Win. Cath., 1976).

Wilson, D. M., ed., *The Architecture of Anglo-Saxon England* (1960).

Wood, R. G. E., County Advisory Officer, History; Essex County Council.

INDEX ONE

by *Grace Holmes*

Persons and Places

INDEX TWO

by *Grace Holmes*

Subjects and Terms

155

158

tenons (cont.)
  free, 135; spur shouldered,
    135
thatch, 43
tie beams: 6, 10, 12, 16, 18,
    20, 21, 22, 26, 27, 28, 29,
    32, 33, 34, 40, 41, 55, 58,
    67, 88, 95, 97, 98, 99, 100,
    101, 102, 103, 105, 106,
    107, 108, 109, 110, 111,
    112, 113, 115, 116, 117,
    118, 119, 120, 121, 122,
    123, 124, 125, 126, 127,
    128, 129, 130, 131, 132,
    133, 134, 135, 137;
    cranked, 116
ties: 104, 134; crenellated,
    107; diagonal, 132; end,
    107; spur, 27, 40, 55, 60,
    106, 113, 122; straight,
    125
timber: bent, 39, 44, 45, 75,
    135; compassed, 6, 13,
    103, 125, 126; curved, 44,
    75; green, 90; longitudinal,
    123; re-curved, 61; s-curved,
    45; ships' 90; straight, 44,
    45, 63, 66, 74, 135; verti-
    cal, 76; wavy, 129. *See also*
    oak; piers; pine; planks; soft-
    wood
towers: 69, 76;
  individual buildings; Blackmore, 46, 69, 76; Bowers
Gifford, 98; Bulphan, 46,
69, 76, 100, Plate XXVIII,
Canewdon, 100; Earls
Colne, 103; Eastwood,
104; Felstead, 105;
Fobbing, 106; Great Dun-
mow, 108; Great Leighs,
108; Great Tey, 109; Great
Waltham, 110; Greensted
juxta Ongar, 110; Hockley,
113; Little Bardfield, 116;
Little Totham, 72-3, 77,
119; Maldon: All Saints,
120; Margaretting, 46, 69,
76, 120; Marks Tey, 74-5,
77, 120; Mundon, 121;
Navestock, 62, 122, Plate
XXI; Rawreth, 125; Ray-
leigh, 125; Rayne, 125;
Stambourne, 129; Stifford,
130; Thorrington, 133;
West Bergholt, 135; West
Mersea, 135; Wickham
St. Paul, 137
tracery: 45, 49, 52, 53, 56,
138; canopied, 31; semi-
103, 107, 113, 118, 122,
128, 129, 130, 134; blind,
53; cinquefoil, 108, 109,
118, 132; quatrefoil, 32,
56, 127; trefoil, 135. *See
also* lights; spandrels

transoms, 62, 64, 69, 102,
    118, 128, 130, 134, 137
tree nails, 7
tree trunks as walls, 1, 43,
    110
trimmers, 135
Tudor period and style, 33,
    36-41, 57, 76, 97, 103,
    108, 111, 115, 119, 122,
    123, 125, 131, 133, 136
tympanums, 79

vergeboards: 47, 53, 57, 97,
    115; cusped, 51, 117, 122
Victorian style and period
    (19th century), 110, 111,
    112, 113, 115, 118, 121,
    124, 125, 129, 130

walls: pieces, 14, 17, 20, 21,
    22, 24, 25, 26, 27, 28, 29,
    32, 34, 37, 40, 66, 69, 88,
    94, 95, 96, 98, 99, 101,
    102, 103, 104, 105, 107,
    108, 109, 110, 113, 115,
    116, 117, 118, 119, 121,
    125, 126, 127, 129, 130,
    131, 132, 133, 136, 137,
    136; canopied, 31; semi-
    octagonal, 33, 37
windows, 1, 2, 8, 32, 41, 43,
    72, 76, 97, 110, 113, 130,
    135